an extraordinary love story

TOTAL PARDON

Wil and Linda Yazzie

With Jodie Randisi

This book is riveting. I had settled in to read Total Pardon and found I couldn't just read a few pages and put it down until later. I had to finish the book. WOW! That's all I can say. What a wonderful book about triumph, courage, and faith. The true meaning of love arises, again and again, to help Wil overcome his addictions. Linda's unconditional love, along with her belief in prayer, is an awesome testament of how true love can overcome all obstacles. This book should be shared, given to family and friends. Wil and Linda are an awesome couple! Bless both of you for writing this awesome book. Very inspiring. It is a must read!

Ynema Pemberton LaFuria

This is one of the best books I have read in my entire life! I read it twice the first day I got it. What a touching love story, and such an amazing testimony to the power and love of God. It is plain to see that God used everything in Wil and Linda's lives, both the good and the bad, to equip them for a powerful ministry. I believe the study guide at the end of the book will be used far and wide to reach those who suffer with drug and alcohol abuse. Thanks for such an informative, exciting book!

Rena Tipton

Words cannot describe this AWESOME book! I don't even like to read but I started reading Total Pardon the day I received the book. I could not put it down. I'm encouraging all my young people to read your book. Thank you, Wil and Linda, for sharing your story with all of us. And most importantly, thank you, GOD, for your unconditional LOVE! **Rebekah Harlow**

I purchased the e-book of Total Pardon the first day it was launched on Amazon but didn't start reading it right away because I was finishing another book. But once I started reading it, I was unable to put it down until I had finished the entire book. I may get the hard copy for my bookshelf. I love true stories that end in triumph!!! **Jenny from TX**

I am so glad Wil and Linda put their story out there for the whole world to read. It will truly save lives. I have a friend who plans on sharing it with some boys she works with. Hopefully, it will change their lives. I know it has changed mine. God bless Linda and Wil! They are both very special people. **Clarrisa Miller**

I thank Jesus for saving Wil from his addictions, and I thank Linda for her prayers and unconditional love for Wil. This is a very powerful book and hits home in many ways. I believe God had this book published at this time so I can send it to my son in jail so he might also see the love of Jesus. Thank you, from the bottom of my heart, for sharing your truly amazing story of love and faith.

Faye (White Dove)

I just finished Total Pardon. WOW!!!! **Jack, New Mexico**

To Jean,
God bless you!
Love in Christ,
Linda + Wil Yazzie
7/24/15

COWCATCHER
publications

ISBN: 978-0982152133
Copyright © 2012, 2015 by Wil and Linda Yazzie with Jodie Randisi
All rights reserved. COWCATCHER PUBLICATIONS
Printed in the United States of America

To Jean!
God bless you!
Love in Christ,
Linda Uribe

What an absolutely a lovely story! No matter what one has done in the past, the faith, belief and trust in the Lord shall make one rise to their fullest potential, that's a fact. So glad you and Linda found each other again. How beautiful is that?
Andrea J Montoya

7/24/15

Contents

1   DEDICATION

3   INTRODUCTION

9   *Chapter One*   CHILDHOOD INTERRUPTED

15   *Chapter Two*   GROWING UP NAVAJO

19   *Chapter Three*   OPEN DOORS OF ANOTHER KIND

25   *Chapter Four*   PLEASING THE ELDERS

29   *Chapter Five*   CAUGHT

33   *Chapter Six*   UNDER THE INFLUENCE

41   *Chapter Seven*   CHILOCCO SCHOOL FOR INDIANS

47   *Chapter Eight*   BREAKING RECORDS AND STUFF

51   *Chapter Nine*   CHRISTMAS IN OCTOBER

55   *Chapter Ten*   CONFINEMENT

59   *Chapter Eleven*   WHAT NOW

63   *Chapter Twelve*   TRAPPED

67   *Chapter Thirteen*   FUGITIVE WANTED

71   *Chapter Fourteen*   ARRESTED AGAIN

77   *Chapter Fifteen*   IT SEEMED RIGHT AT THE TIME

83   *Chapter Sixteen*   COSTLY MISTAKES

89   *Chapter Seventeen*   PEN PALS

93   *Chapter Eighteen*   NOTHING TO LOSE

97 **Chapter Nineteen** DANGEROUS BUT SACRED GROUND

101 **Chapter Twenty** MODEL PRISONER, BAD PAROLEE

113 **Chapter Twenty-One** FAMILIAR SINS

117 **Chapter Twenty-Two** CAN'T GIVE UP

119 **Chapter Twenty-Three** REPEAT OFFENDER

123 **Chapter Twenty-Four** WEAPON OF CHOICE

127 **Chapter Twenty-Five** HOME SWEET HOME

135 **Chapter Twenty-Six** PRINCE NOT SO CHARMING

141 **Chapter Twenty-Seven** WASTED YEARS

147 **Chapter Twenty-Eight** WITHOUT WIL

151 **Chapter Twenty-Nine** GET RID OF HIM

155 **Chapter Thirty** TRANSITIONS

159 **Chapter Thirty-One** ACTING IS AN ART

165 **Chapter Thirty-Two** LAST CHANCE

171 **Chapter Thirty-Three** ALL THESE THINGS

177 **Chapter Thirty-Four** TOTAL FORGIVENESS

183 **Chapter Thirty-Five** RECOVERY

189 APPENDIX A — About The Navajo People

201 APPENDIX B — Substance Abuse on the Reservation

210 DISCUSSION QUESTIONS

an extraordinary love story

TOTAL PARDON

DEDICATION

This is a faithful saying and worthy of all acceptance, that Christ Jesus came into the world to save sinners, of whom I am chief. However, for this reason I obtained mercy, that in me first Jesus Christ might show all longsuffering, as a pattern to those who are going to believe on Him for everlasting life. Now to the King eternal, immortal, invisible, to God who alone is wise, be honor and glory forever and ever.. Amen.

I Timothy 1:15–17

"My name is Wilford Yazzie and I am the worst of sinners."

Like the apostle Paul said, I, too, am the worst of sinners. I was without hope that I would ever be any different or healed from my addictions. In the past, during my years as an addict, I had checked myself into more than twenty different rehab programs. During those years, I would have described myself in the present tense—I am an alcoholic.

In 2005, I repented and surrendered my entire life to Jesus Christ. I became a new person. I was finally done with all my old ways. Since that day, my thoughts have become new thoughts and my habits have become healthy habits. To God be the glory!

Describing my past life for this book was not easy. There are many chapters of my life I would prefer to leave out. I have done things for which I am ashamed. It has been hard for my wife Linda and me to share these stories. But we know that the Lord would have our lives to be an "open book" for others to read. We have a burden for the multitudes of people who are bound by sin. If by sharing our story, we can introduce just one person to Jesus Christ, then our effort will be worth it.

This book is for people who feel hopeless because the enemy has told them there is no way out of addiction. Our hope is that everyone reading this will turn to Jesus Christ. We want readers to know Jesus is the answer. What He did for me—the chief of sinners—He can do for anyone. No matter how low one has sunk into sin and despair there is hope through the precious name of Jesus.

I dedicate this book and our story to all people who are bound by addiction, especially my own beloved Native American people. Linda would like to dedicate this book and our story to her mother, Lucille, her father, Winford Amyx and siblings, Frankie, Jim, Gary, and especially to her sister and best friend, Nancy.

INTRODUCTION

Jodie

But it is good for me to draw near to God; I have put my trust in the Lord GOD, that I may declare all Your works.

Psalm 73:28

How I met Wilford Yazzie is interesting but not all that significant to his life story. Nonetheless, our meeting masterfully sets up a greater story, which I hope will become plain by the end of the book.

Wil and I met in a remote part of the Mojave Desert in June 2007. We were on location shooting a short film. Wil was an actor and I was a screenwriter receiving a hands-on education about the business of filmmaking. The month my husband and I spent in California was a colossal disappointment except for meeting Wil. Now we know it was the Lord who brought us together and it was His master plan that I would uncover and record Wil's story.

Wil had been hired to play the part of a medicine man for a short film called *Legend of Earth and Sky*. He certainly looked the part; his appearance exuded generational, indigenous, Native American wisdom. He needed someone to run lines with him. That's how I came into the picture. I was happy to help.

It didn't take long for Wil and I to become friends. I told him about my student teaching days at Chinle Boarding School in Many Farms, Arizona back in 1979. In one short break, we shared many things. My experience with Bureau of Indian Affairs boarding schools caught his attention. Why would a screenwriter from South Carolina know anything at all about BIA boarding schools in Arizona?

I chose to do my student teaching on an Indian reservation and not in the inner city of Chicago or the mountains of Appalachia. My selection was a rather casual decision. It was my last semester as a college student and going somewhere new and doing something out of the ordinary was the driving force behind my decision. Thirty years later, I have a deeper appreciation for the divine purpose behind my pretty much random choice. I chose an unconventional student teaching program that allowed me the opportunity to live on the Navajo reservation and teach Navajo students.

Within minutes of meeting one another, Wil had to admit I was more familiar with his culture than most Anglos. I told Wil my best reservation story; my dorm-room werewolf-poster blooper. We had a good laugh and then my instinct as a writer kicked in. This guy needed to tell me his story, not the other way around.

"So, Wil, how did you get into acting?" I asked.

"I haven't always been an actor, Jodie," he told me.

"Well, I guess not. Nobody's born an actor."

I could tell by the cadence in his speech that I was conversing with someone who had two languages competing for his tongue. In order to tell me his story, Wil had to clear away some Navajo in favor of English.

"I used to be a homeless," Wil state matter-of-factly. "For most of my life, I was a hopeless alcoholic." He said all that with a twinkle in his eye. I remember thinking, with a beard and a red suit, this guy would make an outstanding Native American Santa

Claus.

"Oh?"

"My street name was Roho. I was an ex-con living on the streets, eating out of garbage cans. But all that changed in 2005." He paused.

"What happened in 2005?" Somehow I knew before he answered that he was about to give me his Christian testimony.

"Some guy saw me passed out on the street. He stopped to talk to me. He said, 'Aren't your people supposed to be warriors? Why aren't you fighting?' Then he told me that Jesus loved me."

"I knew it!" I said exclaimed. "You know how Christians just know when they've met another brother or sister in Christ? I knew we had something in common other than government boarding schools. I want to hear your story, Wil. And start at the beginning."

I had to know, how does a man break free from decades of alcoholism and go from homelessness to Hollywood? I knew immediately I had uncovered a priceless life story. I was looking at a Native American man who had made a remarkably successful transition from street bum to Hollywood actor. Wil and I agreed. His captivating tale was worthy of an audience.

Thinking I was the ideal person to capture and tell his story, I said, "Let me write about you. I've done this before." Wanting to assure him I was capable of following through, I told him about my first book, *Fear No Evil—The Story of Denny Nissley and Christ in Action,* published in 2000. Nissley's book was more of a collection of the street preacher's outrageous stories than an actual memoir.

I knew immediately that meeting Wil Yazzie was a divine appointment. For the second time in my life, I had stumbled upon a Christian with more than a pocketful of radical true stories. I was having a casual chat and making friends with a man who had no time or inclination to sit down and write his memoir. Perfect!

"I'll do good by you. I promise. When I get home and the movie dust settles, I'll work on writing an article and query some publications. We must stay in touch. You'll probably get tired of hearing from me," I said with journalistic delight.

The dust of Hollywood turned out to be more like impossible-to-remove grime, which gave me an excuse not to pursue Wil's story, at least not for a while. I was troubled because I felt I wasn't keeping my promise to my new friend. What I didn't realize was that the Wil Yazzie story had mushroomed exponentially. God was working in ways neither Wil nor I could have imagined (and one of us is a writer with a vivid imagination).

Eventually, things fell into place and I had time to transcribe some of the most amazing true stories I've ever heard. It's a mystery to me how God coordinated events and synchronized schedules with undisputable accuracy over a period of decades to make two unrelated lives intersect so that great things, such as this book, can happen. That is completely beyond my comprehension. However, I do know why He does it. He does it because He loves us.

It took me a long time to understand that the summer of 2007 was not a waste of time, energy and money. When I recognized God's redemptive purpose in what I thought was a huge mistake, I realized no one deserved forgiveness and restoration less than Wil, and it was up to me to tell his story. Wil's behavior in no way warranted mercy, which is the reason his life speaks volumes about God's extraordinary love. God loves us mistakes and all. No matter how repulsive we become, God restores beauty to our lives. When we invite Him to do so, it is our heavenly Father's good pleasure to redeem our messy lives.

As the scribe, my job is to capture images of His Majesty's brilliant artistry. I consider Wil and Linda's multi-dimensional love story to be one of those rare occasions where an extraordinary story has the potential to change a person's eternal destination. Any and all glory goes to our Creator.

May the LORD answer you in the day of trouble;
   may the name of the God of Jacob defend you;
May he send you help from the sanctuary,
   and strengthen you out of Zion;
May he remember all your offerings,
   and accept your burnt sacrifice.   Selah

May He grant you according to your heart's desire,
   and fulfill all your purpose.
We will rejoice in your salvation,
   and in the name of our God we ill set up our banners!
May the LORD fulfill all your petitions.

Now this I know that the LORD saves His anointed;
He will answer him from His holy heaven
   with the saving strength of His right hand.

Some trust in chariots, and some in horses;
   but we will remember the name of the LORD our God.
They have bowed down and fallen;
   but we have risen and stand upright.

Save, LORD!
   May the King answer us when we call.

Psalm 20 (NKJV)

CHILDHOOD INTERRUPTED

 *Jodie*

Train a child in the way he should go, and when he is old he will not depart from it.

Proverbs 22:6

Wil was born in 1946 at home with a midwife and a medicine man present. His was a fairly typical beginning for a young Navajo growing up in the southwest at the time. Wil grew up among brothers, sisters, aunts, uncles, great uncles and aunts, and cousins. Like most traditional Navajo households, his elders spoke only Navajo. Wil's family may have recognized and even used a few common English words or phrases but only in public places and only when communication with Anglos was absolutely necessary.

Life on the reservation was not easy. His parents were seasonal workers. They followed crops. The Yazzies, and every other Native American family Wil had contact with, had to overcome severe economic and social obstacles. However, Wil's childhood had an extra dose of dysfunction.

Three-year old Wil had watched his dad and his buddies get drunk on more than one occasion. When the men weren't working, they were drinking. Still, things had to get done. One summer day in 1949, Mr. Yazzie had orders from Mrs. Yazzie to go fetch supplies, booze and groceries—in that order. Wil remembers feeling lucky. Chosen from the flock of siblings, he was the one who got to leave and go to town with azhé'é, his father.

Getting into a vehicle with a drunk relative behind the wheel is an ongoing problem on Indian reservations, but when Wil was growing up, it was quite common for Native American children to be exposed to these and other dangerous driving situations. A seat belt, for example, would have been a good idea—had there been such a safety feature. In his haste or haze, Wil's father allowed young Wil to climb into the pickup truck on his own.

"Door's not shut, son," Wil remembers his father saying but doing nothing to correct the situation. A partially unlatched passenger door wasn't a problem until Wil's father yanked on the steering wheel too hard. Mr. Yazzie later told the police he was trying to avoid hitting something on the roadway. Instead of slowing down, the hazardous driver's decision to swerve caused his young son to be thrown from the moving vehicle.

Like a piece of unwanted debris, Wil tumbled out of the moving pick-up truck onto a stretch of uneven pavement. His body eventually came to a stop in a ditch, his lacerations filled with highway gravel and grime. To a distant observer, the boy would have resembled remnants of an exhausted tumbleweed. It had to have been by the grace of God that young Wil Yazzie did not wake up by the side of the road. Instead, he woke up bruised and battered in a hospital bed with nurses and doctors there to comfort him.

Given that inebriated parents who drive with young children are not well liked, the medical personnel who cared for Wil that day must have struggled with their personal feelings towards Johnson Yazzie and the reason they were treating his young son. Wil could have easily died. Medical and law enforcement personnel in the region had to cope with the ugly truth that Wil would probably not be the only victim involved an alcohol related accident coming in that week. Native Americans driving while under the influence was (and continues to be) a problem. Thankfully, Wil's damaged body healed quickly.

The Yazzies moved to Shiprock, New Mexico, where Wil attended elementary school and played sports for the Shiprock Braves. Then, like every migrant worker kid, Wil had to switch schools. His father got a job in Cortez, Colorado. At his new school, Wil was one of three Navajo students, making him an irrestible novelty among the Anglo students.

It didn't take long for the student body to begin asking Wil to perform his tribal dances. Wil became an instant celebrity. Seizing the opportunity he saw before him, he started charging admission for the show, which didn't begin until he had fifty cents in his pocket. He then used his earnings to go to the movies and buy Cokes and popcorn for him and his friends.

With plenty of bravado to go along with his intriguing Navajo ways, this future actor discovered he was quite comfortable in the limelight. He had found a place to shine. Even though there were unexpected economic benefits attributed to his Native American heritage, Wil was happy and relieved when his family moved back to the reservation. He savored what he could from his short-term, pop idol status, but he also liked the idea of returning to the safe haven of living among his people.

Moving to the reservation meant Wil would be getting an education at a Bureau of Indian Affairs boarding school. Unfortunately, boarding school days would have lasting repercussions in Wil's case. His first unexpected challenge was a language barrier. "We were not allowed to speak our native language," Wil said referring to himself and his friends who, along with him, were punished for speaking Navajo. It took years for Wil to be able to work through his painful memories of being forced to speak English. If he didn't (or couldn't) formulate the proper words, his teachers smacked his knuckles with wooden rulers. Following the ruler smacking or other such punishment, Wil and the other stubborn Navajo speakers were required to stand in a corner of the classroom, a left-over government tactic to "erase and replace" Indian culture.

"Because I was not a fluent English speaker, many times I had to guess what people were saying," Wil said. "I didn't understand why school officials were forcing me to be someone I was not."

Wil was required to cut his shiny, thick, black hair, something he and other traditional Navajo boys would not have done if given the choice. Apparently, the United States government was in charge of both hairstyles and language. Navajo students had no choice but to assimilate.

For many Navajo families, BIA boarding schools were accepted as a free childcare plan. They dropped their children off in the fall and picked them up in the spring. Students who enjoyed family visits during the school year were the lucky ones. Relatives brought homemade delicacies along with bags of store bought treats. Sometimes parents would attend athletic events and then take children home for the weekend. Wil's report card, though filled with good grades and positive comments, was not enough to earn him family visitations. As his loneliness increased, so did his resentment. Like many of his friends, Wil had to deal with being separated from loved ones for long periods of time.

Boarding school was, at times, a strange battle for Wil. He did what he could to fill the hollow gap his parents had created. Like any normal child, he felt the sting of being left behind by alcoholic parents. When it came to making the best of a bad situation, he developed a system for coping. He surrounded himself with people and kept busy.

Despite unnecessary chastisement and bouts of loneliness, Wil enjoyed school. Without much effort on his part, he gained the attention and respect of his classmates and athletic coaches. A natural athlete, he joined a sports team each season. Flag football, track, basketball or softball—no matter what the sport, Wil excelled in them all. Sports became Wil's outlet.

People took a genuine liking to Wil. He was friendly with the dormitory staff, coaches, and students. Adults noticed and admired the way he took care of the younger students. Like a concerned big brother, he took the little ones under his wing and watched after them. He protected them from older bullies. He had both instinct and aptitude for helping others less fortunate than himself. If his teachers or coaches saw evidence of Wil's intuitive leadership skills, they didn't do much to nurture it. Although he was developing a servant's heart, it would be many years before someone encouraged him to make the most of his gifts.

While Wil was away at school enjoying athletic endeavors and budding friendships, his parents divorced. In the midst of the family turmoil, a social worker decided Wil and his siblings would be better off living with their grandparents on their farm. It wasn't long before Wil's sisters gave up on rural life. Episodes of sexual abuse had taken their toll. Not surprisingly, they took off and went back to Shiprock.

Wil stayed behind and worked through the sweltering summer months. Among his many farm chores, his least favorite was plowing unwilling wrinkles into unyielding dirt with a worn out mule. It was especially aggravating because while he dutifully did what was expected of him, his cousins sat around and watched.

Wil's family life, splintered by divorce and plagued by poverty, suffered greatly. His childhood was far from what most would call happy or normal. His diligence and hard work often went unacknowledged, and because of that, he actually looked forward to going back to boarding school, the place where he would take his first alcoholic drink.

Chapter Two

GROWING UP NAVAJO

For you formed my inward parts; You covered me in my mother's womb...Your eyes saw my substance, being yet unformed. And in your book they all were written, the days fashioned for me, when as yet there were none of them.

Psalm 139:13, 16

*"My name is Wilford Yazzie
and I am a Navajo."*

I was born at home in Phoenix, Arizona in February 1946. I do not know the actual day I was born. My parents only knew my birth date was in February. I later chose February 22nd because it was the birthday of George Washington. I was the fourth child of Johnson and Edna Yazzie. My older sister, Roselyn, had already died. There was another deceased brother between my older brother and me. No one ever talked about him, so I do not even know his name. After me, there were two more sisters and two brothers.

Our parents lived and worked in Phoenix as migrant workers. Native Americans were generally willing to work any job to keep food on the table for them and their children. This was how it was in my family. My earliest memories are of being left alone with my brothers and sisters while our parents were working or out getting drunk. I remember fending for ourselves and being hungry. When our parents finally came home, there was constant fighting between them.

I spent a lot of time being angry with my parents for what they did to their lives and the lives of us kids. Later, I came to understand what they endured. I faced the same demons and addictions that haunted them.

I am thankful my parents were never physically abusive to us. On the other hand, seeing my dad beat my mom was very traumatic. I tried to help my mom even though I was too small to stand up against a drunken dad. He would push me out of the way and continue beating my mom. Sometimes my older brother ran to a neighbor to call the police and then my dad was taken away to jail. We cried. Mom would bail him out of jail and it would be calm and peaceful for a few days. But then it would start all over again. This was the way we lived for the first eight years of my life.

I started school at Washington Elementary while in Phoenix. This was a break from the constant violence in our home. I loved school, especially recess and sports. I went to an integrated school with Caucasians, African Americans, Asians and Native Americans. I remember the first time I saw a black child. I felt his hair. He had the same color of hair as me but it was so different from my hair. I don't remember any prejudices or trouble at our school. We were too busy playing.

Washington Elementary School was about three miles from the John Jacobs Farm and the housing where we lived. There were a lot of Navajos from Arizona, New Mexico, and Utah living and working on the farm. I heard people bragging about making sixty dollars a week. That was a good salary in the 1950's. The farm had acres and acres of grapes, oranges, and grapefruit, which surrounded the housing area. On weekends and vacations, I went out into the fields with my parents and gathered fruit for our own personal use. My friends and I played in the vineyards. After playing, we ate grapes. They were the best grapes we had ever eaten, or least they seemed that way to us kids.

One day in 1951, Mom told us that we were going home. I didn't know what she meant. Phoenix was home to me. I had just started school. I didn't want to leave my friends. But a child has no say, so we went back to my parents' hometown of Shiprock, New Mexico. We stayed with my dad's parents. New surroundings did not do anything to change the circumstances. My parents continued to drink and fight.

My dad got a job in Cortez, Colorado, so once again we moved to a new home. We stayed at my great-uncle's place and I went to school with their two boys. This was an all white school called Downy Elementary. I found a way to earn a little money in Cortez. I performed "Indian dances" for my White friends for a nickel each. Then on Saturdays, my cousins and I went to a movie. One might think I did a lot of dancing to finance our cinematic adventures, but it only cost twenty cents to get into a movie theater on a Saturday afternoon, which meant we had enough for popcorn, candy and soda. Concessions were only five cents each.

My dad lost his job because of his drinking, and so another chapter in my life ended when we moved back to his parents' home in Shiprock. I had to go to the Bureau of Indian Affairs boarding school in Shiprock. My parents left me at boarding school for many months at a time, including weekends and holidays. I was very lonely, proving that even bad parents are better than no parents. Feelings of rejection began to take root in me at this young age.

In 1954 my parents divorced and abandoned my younger siblings at my grandparents' home. Shortly after the divorce, Mom married a Ute Indian and moved to Cortez, Colorado. Meanwhile, my dad married a Navajo woman and moved to Newcomb. Their new lives did not include making a home for their emotionally fragile children.

My grandparents called a social worker, and my younger brothers were taken to a foster home. At the end of the school year, a social worker picked up my younger sister and me and took us to our uncle's home in Sheep Springs, New Mexico. My youngest sister and younger brothers were already living there. My older brother was still living in Cortez with a Christian family. Two months later my sisters ran away and returned to Shiprock. I did not know why they ran away, but later learned my uncle had been accused of sexual abuse. At the time, I was working with my uncle in the mountains. We hauled logs with a horse to help people build homes. It is hard to believe that one so young could work so hard. Thankfully, it only lasted for a summer.

My uncle had three horses, two were used for pulling the wagon and one was used for riding. One day the horses went missing. Even though I was only eight years old, I was sent to find and bring them back home. I decided I would ride one horse and use him to drive the remaining two back. Even though I had no saddle or bridle with me, I attempted to get on the horse. He whirled around and kicked me in the stomach. I could have easily been kicked in the head. I didn't tell anyone about it even though I was in a lot of pain. I knew I would have been told, "Get over it, kid." God was looking out for me—even back then.

As summer was ending, a social worker took me and my brothers back to Shiprock. We were reunited at my aunt's (Dad's sister) home. Before school started, we suffered through another shuffling of homes when we were sent to my great-aunt's on a farm in Shiprock. In the Navajo way, she was considered my maternal grandma. She was of the same clan as we are. This may sound confusing to non-Navajos but clans are very important to us. It is a bond that cannot be broken or violated. Clans on my mother's side are Edge Water Clan (Tabaahi) and Salt Clan (Ashilli). Clans on my father's side are Tangle People (Ta'neeszahnii) and Big Water Clan (Totsohnii).

Despite our Navajo extended family and tight-knit clan system, the Yazzie family was permanently broken. And like Humpty Dumpty, it would never be put together again.

Chapter Three

OPEN DOORS OF ANOTHER KIND

Whoever causes one of these little ones who believe in Me to sin, it would be better for him if a millstone were hung around his neck, and he were drowned in the depth of the sea.

Matthew 18:6

*"My name is Wil Yazzie
and I am a victim of sexual abuse."*

The 1954–55 school year was very traumatic me. It was the year I was sexually abused by a dormitory matron at boarding school. I was nine years old. I thought my dorm mother was a nice lady but she was not. Dorm mother became very attentive to me. She brought me comic books, new clothes and candies. Looking back, I suppose I was starved for the attention of a mother figure.

One day she took me to her bedroom where she undressed and showered in front of me. She also touched me even though I tried to move away. I was innocent. She was not. I was embarrassed and felt ashamed. I kept all of this to myself. I didn't think anyone would believe me. I was also afraid.

Even though I hated the abuse, I still craved the security the boarding school offered. I had already experienced too many traumatic upheavals. At school, I was popular with my peers and could escape all of my sad memories by playing sports. Also, I never went hungry there. A little boy will endure a lot for food and acceptance. I know now that early childhood sexual abuse opened the door for demons to haunt me.

Unthinkable Punishment

Another part of boarding school that was very painful for me was being punished for speaking Navajo. Today this would be unthinkable. But in the 1950's, Navajo children were not allowed to embrace our culture. Worst of all was how we were punished for speaking Navajo. We were struck with rulers or yardsticks, made to scrub hallways, pick up outdoor trash, and forced to stand in a corner for hours.

This rule was not just enforced in the classroom where it could be argued that it was necessary since the teachers were Anglo and couldn't speak our language. Unfortunately, it was also the rule in our dormitories. The dormitory staff was mostly Navajo, and even though they could speak Navajo, students could not. Also, our hair was cut short as soon as we entered boarding school. We were told cutting hair was the only way to control a potential lice problem. I believe they cut our hair to help us assimilate into the Anglo culture. Because of situations like these, I had trouble trusting the adults in my life.

I believe my experiences at boarding school help explain why I felt and did certain things growing up. For example, my great-uncle, or grandfather in the Navajo way, was a traditional medicine man. Over the summer months, he took me to ceremonies and taught me the traditional ways of our culture. He allowed me to become his helper and I was very happy to be accepted by him. I felt special—a feeling I desperately craved.

I enjoyed being around the elders and listening to their stories and learning the wisdom of our Navajo ways. What little Christian faith I had learned as a child quickly disappeared. I did not realize that by practicing traditional ways I had opened myself up to even more evil spirits.

Encountering the Spirit World

My first real encounter with evil spirits happened one night at boarding school. Like most kids, my roommates and I ignored the "no talking after lights out" rule. We told stories or jokes after "lights out" even though the whole room would be punished if the culprits were caught.

One night, after sharing scary stories with each other, I could not sleep. As I lay in bed, a figure in black suddenly appeared beside my bed. I studied the figure standing by my bed. I could see his face but its body was shrouded in darkness. He was smiling at me and his finger was beckoning me to come to him. I was so frightened I covered my face with my blanket. I didn't move for quite a long time. Finally, I fell asleep.

After that terrifying night, I became afraid of the dark. The image of that shadowy figure continued to haunt me, even into my adulthood. Years later, when I was in prison, I was became fearful after "lights out."

The manifestation of that demon was not my childish imagination. It was very real. People who live on the reservation are afraid at night because of such demonic activity. Many Navajos allow these beliefs to control them.

I was fourteen years old when I had my first contact with a demonic spirit outside of boarding school. I was walking home from my cousin's house and felt a strange presence with me just as I was walking across a bridge. I heard footsteps but when I turned around there was no one there. I started walking and turned around when I again heard more footsteps. I went back to where I heard the sound but no one was there. I realized that a spirit was there with me and we had started playing a game of hide 'n seek.

At first, it was kind of fun. We played until I got to the end of the bridge. I didn't realize at the time who or what I had allowed into my life. In reality, I had invited evil spirits to hang around me. There is no such thing as fun and games with Satan or his demons. I found out that once unleashed, demons play for keeps.

A few months later, I had another experience with the spirit world while walking home from the same cousin's place in Shiprock. We had been watching football on television. Since we had no electricity on the farm, watching television was a big deal for me. I lost track of time. By the time I started home, it was cold and dark. I stopped to rest in a shed by a towing garage. I was almost asleep when I heard voices in Navajo saying, "Is he asleep yet?"

I thought it was someone trying to pull a prank on me. I jumped up and ran around the shed. There was no one there or in the surrounding vicinity. Thinking it was my imagination, I laid back down. I heard the voices again, this time in English. "Is he asleep yet?" I realized it was a spirit bothering me, so I ran to the nearby police station. I spent the rest of the night there sleeping on a couch in the lobby.

By the age of fourteen, evil spirits had their hooks in my heart and mind. I wanted to escape my fears, hurts and disappointments. Satan and his demons were there to help me. As a result, I made many wrong choices that led to multiple addictions. I was primed and ready to do their biding and I had many like-minded supporters along the way to encourage me.

Like many of my friends, I respected our traditional Navajo customs. I accepted the spirit world as normal. However, because I had not known anything but rejection and trauma in my young life, I felt unloved and alone. I had been forced to go to church when at boarding school but knew nothing about the love of Jesus Christ. Christianity was something the "White people" told us about. I had no idea of how to resist the temptations of Satan.

No Escaping Superstitions or Satan's Traps

Too many Navajo live in a world of fear because of superstitions. The proof is in the fact that so many Navajos are bound by fear of the medicine men, skinwalkers and animals. They escape these fears through alcohol and drugs. Domestic violence and child abuse (both physical and sexual) is rampant on the reservation. I know because I experienced all of it. However, I have found that traditional ways do not bring comfort or peace. It is quite the opposite. Today I walk in the Light and all my fears have been banished. I know that God protects me and is with me.

When I was a young boy I made a vow that I would never drink. Even as a child I knew alcohol had destroyed our family. I felt resentment, anger and hatred toward drunken adults, especially my relatives. What I didn't realize was that a spiritual battle for my soul had begun. I was easy prey for Satan. He set a trap for me. Actually, he set many traps for me, none of which a vow could stop.

Chapter Four

PLEASING THE ELDERS

 *Wil*

For the love of money is a root of all kinds of evil, for which some have strayed from the faith in their greediness, and pierced themselves through with many sorrows.

I Timothy 6:10

*"My name is Wil and when I was a child,
I wanted to please my elders."*

I became addicted to gambling at a young age. Gambling was a regular event at my grandmother's home. The elders and people from Utah, Arizona and Colorado came to my grandmother's home to gamble. I wanted to be a part of their world so I gambled with them. I was twelve years old and very good at card games. I worked on the neighbors' farms for money so I could gamble. I worked all day for five dollars to play poker. In those days, we used horses to work the farmland. It was especially hard work for one so young.

Sometimes I lost money but mostly I won. The elders would get upset when I won but I enjoyed beating them. When I won, I bought soda pop or candy for my brothers and sisters. There were three families living with us. Even though my grandma received financial help for keeping my siblings and me, we benefited very little. It seemed there was never enough food to go around at my grandma's house. The adults grabbed most of the food. It was hard for me to see my brothers and sisters go hungry. At every meal, we were told to eat last. I didn't mind for myself as much as I did for them. Providing treats for my siblings was my motivation for gambling. This is how I justified my actions.

My heart was becoming hard. I was angry that my uncle got paid every month but would just drink it up. My great-uncle/grandpa got checks from social security and was also paid for his medicine man duties, but his money went to drinking as well. He thought only of himself. His children got more food than me and my brothers and sisters. When I would argue and accuse my elders of eating the food paid for with money received for our support, my grandma would get angry with me. She took up for her brother and his children. This only made me more resentful and angry. I could not understand why my family was always last. Why were we never loved?

Another Vices Takes Root

To support my growing gambling addiction, I began stealing. I needed more and more money to gamble because I was hooked. My life of stealing began years earlier when I went into a store with my aunt. She put items in my pockets and told me to keep quiet and walk out of the store. I went back into the store and she would put more small items into my pockets or into a sack that she gave me to carry.

It wasn't until I was fourteen years old that I stole without any influence from an adult. I remember the first item I stole on my own. A few of my friends and I went to an Anglo home in Shiprock where we stole a bicycle. I wanted this bike because I had always dreamed about owning one. I later regretted this decision because it almost resulted in my death.

I had been away from home for a few days because I stayed over at a friend's house. When I returned home, my uncle was very angry with me. He was upset because I did most of the work around the farm. Chores were left undone in my absence. He was so angry and drunk that he got in his car and tried to run me over with it. I pedaled as fast as I could but I could not outrun a car. He destroyed the bike, but God, in His loving mercy, protected me.

This was not the first time my life was spared. I have memories. When I was three years old I fell out of my dad's pick up truck, but God was with me. When I was about four years old, a drunken uncle was angry for some reason and took it out on me. I was very afraid and ran out of the house to hide in a nearby orchard. Unfortunately, he saw me and came after me. He picked me up and threw me as hard as he could. He did that repeatedly until a neighbor rescued me. Again, I suffered bruises and cuts but miraculously escaped serious injury.

Meanwhile, my life as a thief continued to escalate. It was more than just being able to get easy money. I felt a sense of power over people when I was stealing. At night, I would get together a group of my friends and take them to the boarding school. I showed them how to pry open windows and doors. Once inside, we stole food, radios and any small items that would be easy to sell. This would continue for two years.

Liquor Store Regular

There was another reason I stole. Not only was I addicted to gambling, but I had also started to drink heavily. I promised myself that I wouldn't be like my alcoholic parents, but when I was in junior high school, I went to a liquor store off the reservation and bought some wine with stolen funds. I drank until I passed out. I enjoyed passing out.

When I woke up, I still had money. As soon as I was sober, I returned to the liquor store to buy more. My life as an alcoholic had begun and would continue for the next forty-four years. Although I did not want it to be, my life was controlled by hatred and anger, which I tried to smother with alcohol. The years of neglect and abuse opened more doors for even more demons I was angry at the world. I wanted to make someone pay for my hurts, only I was the one who paid the price..

CAUGHT

 *Wil*

The rod and rebuke give wisdom, but a child left to himself brings shame to his mother.

Proverbs 29:15

*"My name is Wil
and I was a disgrace to my mother."*

My life of crime had begun when I became desperate for money. I needed to feed my addictions. My friends and I came up with a plan. We went to a hotel in Shiprock where we knew the phone was located away from the clerk's counter. One friend would call the desk manager from the pay phone in the hotel restaurant. While she was away on the phone, I opened the cash register and stole the money in the cash drawer. We did this several times. I gave my friends money for helping, but I kept the majority of the cash since I considered myself the brains of our little gang. I needed a sense of empowerment to boost my fragile self-image.

I was also caught stealing from several different stores and gas stations around Shiprock and Farmington. Our life of crime was about to come to an abrupt end. My luck had run out.

Youth Offenders Go to Prison

I latched on to the old saying that there is honor among thieves. When I was arrested, I refused to tell on my friends and took the rap myself. After spending a night in the Shiprock jail, I was transferred to the Aztec County Jail where I stayed for one week. The lady next to my cell gave me cigarettes and candy to calm me down when she heard me crying. This is when I accepted another bad habit—smoking. It was like boarding school all over again. I had no family visitors or anyone to help me.

After my one-week stay at the Aztec County Jail, a federal marshal from Albuquerque took me to a juvenile hall. I was locked up with youthful offenders my age or older. A month later, I went to court and was sentenced to one year at the Federal Correctional Institute for Youth in Englewood, Colorado. Some of my friends were already at the FCI when I arrived. It was like a homecoming for me.

When I arrived I heard shouts of "Roho! Roho!" Roho was my street nickname. It means "red" in Spanish. The term actually came from a song about a red rooster.

Out of seven hundred juveniles at this facility, only two of us were fifteen years old. Taking care of myself was not a problem. I enjoyed fighting. My new environment was meant to be educational. I learned some trade skills and also picked up tricks of the criminal kind. I enjoyed making things grow and being outside the prison fences was better than being stuck inside, so I took landscaping classes. I continued to gamble, only instead of winning money I won cigarettes, candy and snacks. Looking back, my experience at FCI was both good and bad.

I went before the parole board after six months but was told I had to complete my sentence of ten months. When the time came for my release, I was taken by the guards to downtown Denver and put on a bus to Shiprock. There was no one to meet me at the bus depot because I didn't tell my family I was coming home. I hadn't seen them for over a year and I knew they wouldn't care. My first stop was the liquor store in Hogback. When I arrived back at the farm, I was drinking.

My relatives enrolled me in Shiprock Junior High School, but by this time, I had added the use of marijuana to my list of vices. My old friends were still at Englewood so no one in Shiprock knew I had been in a federal reformatory. However, my days of playing in basketball and running track were over. I was now moving in different circles.

I went back to stealing. I would go into stores and the bus depot to steal money and turquoise jewelry. One day, my cousin and I met some girls who wanted to party. We didn't have any money but they had a car. So I came up with a plan involving a Conoco gas station. While the attendant was busy putting gas in the tank and checking the oil, I went to the cash register and stole everything in it. We used to hang around with the attendant so he knew who we were. When he discovered the missing cash, he called the police. The hunt for us was on.

Hiding in Freezing Water

My cousin was caught first. When I realized the police were after me, I hid the money in some bushes and crawled into a creek to hide. I stayed there all night. The water was very cold at first, but after a while, the water began to seem warm. I could hear the police walking all around. I was hidden from their view by the bushes in the embankment. When I had the chance, I took a quick look and saw the police still searching, so I crawled back into my hiding place and stayed there until early morning.

By morning, I was freezing cold and muddy. I came out of the creek to go to my cousin's house. I passed one house and a friend called out, "Hey Roho! The police are looking for you." I realized then that the authorities knew who I was and my chances of escaping were not good. I continued to my cousin's house. His father told me that my cousin was already in jail. After I told him what happened, he gave me dry clothes and told me to leave but to watch after myself.

I retrieved some of the stolen money and found a friend who bought me a jacket and two bus tickets. Our plan was to go to Farmington where we could resume drinking. My friend was old enough to legally buy alcohol. As soon as we got to Farmington, we got drunk. I lost him somewhere in town and decided to hitchhike back to Shiprock where a cousin picked me up and took me back to the farm. My grandmother told me the police were looking for me. I told her what happened and that I wanted to run away to Phoenix, but she and my uncle convinced me to surrender to the police. They took me to the Shiprock jail.

The next day the FBI agent from Farmington came and talked to me. I took him to where I had stashed the stolen money. We had spent of the money in Farmington and some of it had blown away. The FBI was able to recover a good portion of it. I was released to my grandmother's care with a warning; I had to be enrolled in the Chilocco Indian School in Oklahoma.

Peers Were Not the Problem

Grandmother was sure that getting away from my peers in Shiprock would help me. She didn't realize that the problem was within me and no change of address or friends would put me on a different path. By this time, the demons associated with alcoholism were controlling my thoughts.

There was only one person who could save me from addiction but I wasn't ready to surrender to Jesus Christ. I was my own little god. I thought I was still in control of my life.

Chapter Six

UNDER THE INFLUENCE

 *Jodie*

For I know that in me (that is, in my flesh) nothing good dwells; for to will is present with me, but how to perform what is good I do not find. For the good that I will to do, I do not do; but the evil I will not to do, that I practice. Now if I do what I will not to do, it is no longer I who do it, but sin that dwells in me..

Romans 7:18–20

Wil was in the eighth grade when he took his first sip of alcohol. He drank until he passed out. When he woke up, he took off to find his new drinking buddies so he could do it again. He was an alcoholic right from the start. Something clicked. Once initiated into the world of drinking, Wil was hooked.

For most people, suffering the normal after effects of consuming too much alcohol is enough to help them quit drinking, at least for a couple of months, sometimes years. Not Wil. Wil did not experience the usual symptoms of a first time alcohol abuser. He didn't get sick or wake up with an unbearable hangover. He was able to go to school the next day where he took advantage of the opportunity to steal money so he could get drunk again. This time he paid for everyone to pass out and his popularity among Student Drinkers skyrocketed.

Booze Blankets, Benders and Blackouts

Wil was not just an underage drinker. He was a full-fledged teenaged alcoholic. Benders and blackouts were the norm. He drank until he forgot how much he had already drank, and then he drank some more. He found out early that a booze blanket temporarily warmed a cold and lonely situation. It was easier to retreat into the nothingness of a drunken stupor than to confront challenges. Alcohol quite easily became Wil's master, telling him what to do and how to do it.

Becoming addicted to alcohol was not what Wil had imagined for himself. The constant abuse of alcohol, much of which occurred in and around Wil's home, had him convinced another path would be a more desirable choice. As a child growing up, he had told himself many times that he would not follow in the footsteps of his parents and drunken uncles, yet that is exactly what he did. Apparently, exposure didn't induce abstinence.

Wil's early alcohol abuse grew like an ugly germ. The infectious bug received constant nurturing because it had been planted under peak conditions. It's no wonder things got out of control so quickly. Letting go of inhibitions and forgetting how poorly life had treated him became an attractive and compulsive thing to do. An alcoholic stupor was better than harsh memories of being tossed around like garbage or getting run over by a car while riding a bike. For Wil, there were no genies in bottles waiting to grant him happy wishes. There were only greedy demons fueled with wicked desires of their own.

In between going to school and sports practices, Wil found

the time and courage to go with friends to the liquor store. His downward spiral had begun. Without concerned adults or caring family to intervene, his decline flourished. He knew he was running with the wrong crowd but went anyway. It was routine Indian reservation mischief—everyone did it and nobody cared about consequences. Most Navajo youth had no future plans to hold onto, which meant they were free to be as bad and daring as they cared to be.

No Longer a Bystander

Making friends with a guy with a driver's license and a car was a plus for Wil. Stealing money to purchase beer, wine and gas was easier now that the gang had a go-to guy in their crew. Getting everyone back to Shiprock where they could get drunk without the watchful eye of boarding school staff was the plan—until someone got the bright idea to steal what remained of the stolen money. Young and stupid drunk, things were bound to get out of control, as they often did. Wil was drawn into the dispute of who stole what. Drunken tempers and violent outbursts were the norm, especially at night on the reservation. Wil had seen it all before but from a distance. Things had changed. Wil was no longer an innocent bystander.

In time, Wil's schemes for coming up with drinking money failed him—as did the judicial system. Over the years, various officials, whose duty it was to administer appropriate punishment, made more than a few bad choices. Perhaps they had better and more important things to do. Wil and his buddies were often sent home or back to school with a just warning.

Eventually, one of Wil's many misdemeanors finally caught up with him and he did find himself behind bars. Being arrested was a bit of a shock. It was enough to start a new habit, another vice with a price. He was fifteen years old when someone offered him a smoke. Without anyone to tell him that smoking cigarettes is highly addictive and increases a person's risk of getting lung cancer, emphysema and bronchial disorders, Wil became a smoker.

No big deal. Smoking was part of growing up. Everyone did it, including student athletes.

Wil's time in local jail was followed by an appearance before a judge. Not willing to rat out his friends, Wil confessed, "Your Honor, I did it." Upon his confession, he was hauled off to the Aztec County Jail in Farmington where he stayed for a week until a United States Marshal from Albuquerque came and got him. The judge in Albuquerque sentenced Wil to one year at a federal reformatory in Englewood, Colorado where he lived with other juvenile offenders.

In a sense, Wil was fortunate. Six months into his sentence, Wil had a parole hearing. His request was denied but he was able to finish his sentence in his own cell in the honor dorm. He was free to lift weights and talk with friends. He learned how to play cards and gambled for cigarettes among other things. He played Ping Pong and became good at keeping busy. Wil Yazzie enjoyed the feeling of solidarity and acceptance among the other juvenile delinquents. He finished his sentence peacefully. But then he got out.

Old Habits, New Friends

Incarceration had little effect on Wil. It didn't take long for Wil to pick up old habits once he arrived in Shiprock. If Wil had been even a little bit sensible, he would have entertained the thought that perhaps his life was starting to implode.

Relationships based on booze break down inhibitions and cross all tribal lines, which is why in 1961, when he and his cousin Sandy caught a ride with a couple of wild Indian girls, they were talked into stealing money from a gas station.

With two girls and an offer to go bar hopping, Sandy and Wil, who now went by Roho, could not refuse. Armed with a couple of six packs of Budweiser for the road, the newly formed gang of four hopped in the car and drove to Hogback, New Mexico.

When they arrived, the girls disappeared into a well-known local hangout, the Turquoise Bar. They emerged a half hour later excited to tell Roho and Sandy about the plan they had hatched to get more drinking money. The plan was to stop at a full-service gas station where the girls would distract the attendant as he washed the windshield and checked the oil. Roho's job was to go inside and grab whatever he could from the cash register, a task he was already familiar with doing. Robbing a gas station convenience store to ensure non-stop intoxication didn't seem dangerous, nor did it pose much of a threat to the blissfully ignorant band of inebriated teens.

Just as Roho grabbed a bundle of bills, the girls sped off in the car. With no other options, Sandy and Roho took off runniing. This was not part of the plan—or was it? The search for the Conoco gas station robbers began when the attendant called the cops. Police officers were in the vicinity. With the police closing in, Roho decided it would be best to get rid of the cash, which was the only evidence that a crime had been commited. As he ran through a field headed for safety in the outskirts of town, he tossed the bundle of cash. He didn't know there was an imposing obstacle in his way. He was headed straight for a creek.

Icy Asylum

Determined to remain free, Roho took refuge in the icy cold creek. Using a rock for a pillow, he stayed submerged in the frigid creek water throughout the entire night because he discovered he could breathe without moving or attracting attention. Roho's face was the only part of his body above water. Limbs from scrub brushes helped to conceal his watery hiding place.

Although he may not have realized it at the time, Wil's icy asylum had brought on Roho's first case of hypothermia. Roho had escaped both police arrest and premature death that night. If he had not left the creek when he did, he might have died a Hogback popsicle.[1] Somehow, early the next morning, Roho overcame the effects of the bitter cold and went back to get the money.

---

1   "Popsicle" is the term authorities use to describe people, usually drunken Indians or homeless bums, who black out and then die outside in the cold.

After a few days on the run, Roho ended up at a friend's house. With something akin to brotherly love with a twist of addiction, Roho's friend gave him a jacket, money for a warm coat and a bus ticket to Farmington where "they could get their drink on." After an extended drinking spell in Farmington, Roho became separated from his friend. He caught a ride back to Shiprock where his grandmother told him in Navajo, "The police are..."

"The police are looking for me. I know," he told her in English.

His grandmother and uncle convinced him to turn himself in to the authorities. The idea sounded good to Wil; the spartan appeal of evading law enforcement had worn off. Wil was driven to the Shiprock tribal police station to face his accusers. The plan was to tell the authorities that his criminal behavior was due to the fact he was out-of-his-mind drunk. When they asked what he did with the money, he told them. From the back seat of a police car, Wil was asked to confirm the approximate location of the loot, after which the FBI found the cash and Wil went back to jail.

Sentenced to Chilocco School for Indians

A judge let Wil return to grandmother's farm on the condition that he enroll in the Chilocco Indian School in Oklahoma.[2] If he did, he would not face prosecution for the gas station robbery. Wil liked the idea of going back to being a student. He actually looked forward to not being a fugitive, getting off the streets and settling down.

At Chilocco, students were exposed to all kinds of trades and practical vocational skills that would significantly increase their chances of developing an honorable livelihood after graduation, a rare privilege for most Native Americans. Agriculture, horseshoeing, blacksmithing, building trades, printing, shoe repair, tailoring, leather work, homemaking, cooking, and in later

---

2   The Chilocco Indian School provided vocational education and training to Native Americans from across the U.S. for nearly 96 years. The school closed its doors in 1980 but not because they had run out of students to serve. The school closed because Congress was advised that the cost per student was too high. The actual cost of closing Chilocco Indian School is another story.

years, plumbing, electrical work, welding, auto mechanics, food services and secretarial education were specialty subjects offered at Chilocco. When school was not in session in the summer, many students stayed on and worked in various jobs required to maintain the school and its campus. Chilocco was one place Wil might have thrived had his past not caught up with him.

Wil was enjoying school right up until the day the FBI showed up in Band class. Despite the former agreement made in Shiprock, the gas station robbery case had been reopened. Wil spent the next six days in the Oklahoma City jail, once again waiting for a marshal from Albuquerque to come get him while the legal proceedings of his case were officially determined. As it turned out, Wil spent another month at the Federal Corrections Institute in Colorado. Only this time he wasn't housed in the honor dormitory.

Wil finally had his day in court. The judge asked, "Do you want to go to school?"

"Yes sir," Wil answered. "School helps me stay out of trouble."

The judge sent him back to Chilocco with a stern warning.

"Better behave yourself. Don't drink," the judge said.

"I won't, Your Honor," Wil promised. But he lied. The minute he was offered a sip of alcohol he stopped caring about everyone and everything that meant anything to him.

Chapter Seven

CHILOCCO SCHOOL FOR INDIANS

He who trusts in his own heart is a fool, but whoever walks wisely will be delivered.

Proverbs 28:26

"My name is Wil Yazzie and I am drunk with the power of my popularity and sports abilities."

Native Americans from tribes all across the country went to Chilocco School for Indians. I arrived in August 1962. At that time, Native American tribes did not get along with each other. The Navajos were especially hated because we retained our culture and language. Other tribes had already assimilated into the Anglo culture. All that changed after the Wounded Knee uprising in 1972. This is when the tribes became united in a common cause, Native American civil rights.

I had not regularly attended school since I was in seventh grade. At Chilocco, I was enrolled as a sophomore even though I wasn't. I did well in all my classes even though I was shy and did not participate in class. I did not want to speak in front of people so I never raised my hand. I coasted along and was able to maintain good grades.

On the other hand, I excelled in sports. Any shyness I had was lost on the playing field. I forgot about myself and concentrated on beating the competition on the basketball court or the track field. I played the defensive safety position on the football team, but Oklahoma winters were too harsh for me so I quit halfway into the season.

Due to my athletic abilities, I became very popular with other students from various tribes. A Shoshone girl from Wyoming became my girlfriend. I was shy and had trouble communicating with her. I felt inadequate because I spoke Navajo for most of my life. It was difficult for me to speak fluently in English. English was the language I spoke only when it was necessary, like when speaking to teachers or police officers.

The FBI Finds Me

After I had been in Chilocco for several months, another FBI agent showed up to talk with me about the gas station robbery. He took me to Ponca City where I stayed for one day until a marshal from Oklahoma City came and took me to the Oklahoma City jail. I was there for a week and put in a cell with an Anglo youth from Indiana. I was angry and took my frustrations out on this unfortunate boy. I am ashamed to say that I beat him up and enjoyed it.

I returned to the Federal Correctional Institute in Colorado where I stayed for one month until I was taken to a judge's office. The judge gave me a choice. I could either return to Chilocco or go to a school in Shiprock. I chose to return to Chilocco. I really liked it there. Maybe it was the sports or having the security of a home-like environment. Perhaps it was because of my Shoshone girlfriend. I now believe the Lord was guiding my steps even though I didn't know it at the time. If I had returned to Shiprock, I might have been killed. For an alcoholic thief like me, life was more dangerous in Shiprock.

As soon as I returned to Chilocco, I immersed myself in sports, yet I somehow managed to spend most of my sophomore year drunk. I finished out the school year and came home to Shiprock for the summer to work on the farm. Even though I was drinking, I managed to stay out of trouble with the authorities. I couldn't wait for summer to be over so I could get back to school.

Big Man on Campus

At last August came and I returned to Chilocco. As a junior, I thought I was the big man on campus. And for the first time in my life, I felt a sense of success. I began to think that I might be able to realize my potential. I wanted to go the 1968 Olympics and compete in track and field events. I even started to dream that after graduation I could join my older brother at Brigham Young University in Provo, Utah. Like many teenagers caught in the trap of poverty, I thought sports would be the best and only way out of trouble.

But Satan had other plans for me. In my junior year, the anger in my heart had boiled over into rage. At the time, I was not afraid of anyone or anything. I didn't care about people, including myself. Not even going to jail deterred me from getting into trouble again. My heart was already hardened. Anger was the driving force behind most of my emotions and alcohol fueled all my emotions.

I was an alcoholic and refused to admit it. I considered myself a party animal, not a drunk. I honestly believed I could stop at any time. After all, I was doing well at school and had aspirations of becoming an Olympic athlete. Satan must have been laughing very hard. While I had dreams, he had a pack of lies for me to believe.

Expelled!

Even though I attacked a dormitory attendant, I was allowed to complete my junior year. In the summer, I returned to my hard life on the farm in Shiprock. The thought that I would be starting my senior year soon made the days fly by. Then I received a letter from Chilocco telling me that I had been expelled due to my violent behavior. I was furious. The news of my expulsion escalated my desire to drink. My anger intensified and I became bitter. I had an opportunity to go to other schools, but didn't. Instead, I spent most of my days in Hogback, the nearby town where Navajos went to drink.

One day in early winter, a cousin who was working in Pagosa Springs, Colorado lumber mill, picked me up and took me with him to the mill. I got a job at the lumber mill but quit after two weeks. After my cousin and I got paid, we left Colorado and headed straight for Shiprock. We spent our entire paychecks on liquor, of course.

It didn't take long to figure out that a paycheck and liquor will introduce you to friends you never knew you had. So when my cousin and I arrived at a dance and met up with some "friends," I paid for everyone to get into the dance. I stayed in the car to finish off a bottle or two. My plan was to join them later.

A Fire Build by the Devil

It was a bitter cold night. Sleet was falling from the sky covering everything with a slick wetness. In my altered state of mind, I got out of the car and started walking. I had no idea where I was even though I knew the area like the back of my hand. At some point, I passed out and woke up so cold that it felt as if my joints were frozen. I couldn't move. I saw a fire a short distance away.

The only thought in my mind was to get to that fire and get warm, but as I crawled toward the fire and reached for it, the flames moved. The fire appeared to jump back to where I'd just been. I could feel the warmth of the fire and just wanted to lie down and go to sleep inside its warmth. Somehow, even in my confused state, I could hear the words of my grandmother.

"When people are about to freeze to death, they see a fire, but it is a fire built by the devil," she warned.

The remembrance of her words made me not want to lie down. I started to pray and the first words out of my mouth were, "Jesus, help me! I am about to freeze to death!"

All of a sudden I felt something cover the top of my head. The feeling moved down my entire body to my feet and I was instantly sober. And I knew where I was. My clothes were soaking wet from lying on the ground. I hurried to my great-uncle's house and banged on the door. He took me in and gave me dry clothes and a place to lie down. I received warmth from his fire.

I know now Jesus Christ spared my life that night. He used the words of my grandmother to deliver me from my second case of hypothermia. This was my fourth near death experience but it was the first time I had called upon the name of Jesus. Even though I was shown great mercy and will always remember this incident, I forgot all about my Saviour the very next day. Jesus Christ did not fit into my rebellious life. I turned my back on everything that did not involve alcohol.

Chapter Eight

BREAKING RECORDS AND STUFF

 *Jodie*

Whoever has no rule over his own spirit is like a city broken down, without walls.

Proverbs 25:28

When it came to running, Wil was far better at track and field events than he was at running from the law. After the judge handed Wil a sentence of three years probation, he ordered him back to Chilocco. A few weeks later, he broke a state record in track.

Wil was a popular guy on campus, the basketball court, the football field, and of course, on the dance floor at school dances. In bits and pieces, his future looked bright and promising. On the surface, he appeared to be a one of those well-liked students with an unconscious aptitude to excel. If some adult (a coach, for example) would have mentored and monitored him more carefully, perhaps Wil would have risen to the occasion and made better use of his talents.

Even though getting caught drinking would have been a violation of the terms of his probation, Wil couldn't resist joining his teammates one night on the 39 mile bus trip to Winfield, Kansas. Like most high school basketball teams in the central plains, Chilocco had to travel a good distance to play away games. For whatever reason, the coach who caught the student athletes drinking beer and whiskey did not turn them in. Getting caught would not have discouraged Wil from drinking. His name on a plaque for breaking the state record didn't keep him from drinking. The fact that he had a criminal record didn't matter much either. When it came to drinking or running, Wil surpassed even his own expectations.

After the school year was over, Wil returned to New Mexico to work on the family farm. It was grueling hard work, cutting alfalfa, harvesting corn, and plowing fields with horses—not tractors. Grandfather took all the money for their crops, which meant Wil worked for no pay. He couldn't wait to go back to school.

Back to school meant back with his drinking buddies, constant partying and fistfights with boys from other tribes. Wil couldn't understand why they didn't like each other. The punishment for fighting was being assigned extra chores, which ended abruptly when Wil assaulted a dorm attendant. Wil's altercation with the school staff member resulted in a formal of expulsion from the Chilocco Indian School.

You Are Not Welcome Here

"You are not welcome here," the letter said, adding to Wil's growing list of painful rejections.

Constantly drinking, Wil's life was spinning out of control. Wil had run out of friends. He got the idea that hitchhiking to Gallup where his older brother was living would be the thing to do. Once he got there, he convinced his brother to buy him a bus ticket so he could go back to Oklahoma. Wil thought he could sweet-talk the administrators into trusting him one more time. He thought they might give in because his older brother had been such a model student and was so well liked by the school's superintendent.

When Wil arrived on campus, he somehow managed to stay hidden inside the boy's dormitory for two weeks while he used his charms to persuade administrators to change their minds about him. After much discussion and consternation, they relented. Once again, Wil was enrolled as a student at Chilocco, but it didn't last long. He was only there for one semester. The week before Christmas break Wil got drunk and broke a lot of windows. Shattered glass, shattered dreams.

"You are a person of bad influence. You must leave and you must never come back," they informed Wil.

Wil knew his school years were over for good. He packed up his things and headed for Arkansas City, Kansas, a town seven miles north of Chilocco. This is where and when he took up with some homeless hobos and his childhood ended. It was 1966 and the prospect of a satisfying life had been demolished by yet another self-induced drunken rampage.

Chapter Nine

CHRISTMAS IN OCTOBER

⬛ *Jodie* ⬛

*But Jesus said, "Let the little children come to Me, and do
not forbid them; for of such is the kingdom of heaven."*

Matthew 19:14

Linda Amyx was four-years old and not expected to live. In
October 1954, a well-respected physician told Linda's parents that
she might not make it to Christmas. Mr. and Mrs. Amyx had a
decision to make. They had to decide whether or not they should
give Linda her Christmas presents early that year.

Linda's sore throat turned out to be strep throat. Her condition
worsened until she was diagnosed with full-blown rheumatic
fever. As a result, Linda's heart sustained serious damage. Her
condition was so tenuous that some painful questions had to be
addressed. How long could she survive while her heart pounded
140 times a minute instead of the usual 85 times? Could young

Linda outlive the disease, or would her disease be the victor? In the 1950s, the only known cure for rheumatic fever was bed rest. A solid year of bed rest was Linda's only hope. Heart damage put her life in danger many times, yet her amazing will to live sustained her through several more attacks of rheumatic fever.

During her long confinement, the cheerful little girl had no choice but to put her imagination to good use, which is why her mother did not know what to think when one day that fall Linda told her, "Jesus came to see me last night."

The young shut-in's grave diagnosis necessitated that her announcement be considered, which is why Mrs. Amyx listened carefully as Linda explained the details of her heavenly visit.

"Jesus picked me up and put me on the bed," Linda said. "He told me he wasn't going to take me home yet."

For the parents of a seriously ill child, the image of a child in the arms of Jesus had to be an intensely beautiful thought. Perhaps the Lord had granted their daughter a comforting dream. But as Linda continued to talk about her friend Jesus, Mr. and Mrs. Amyx had to consider the possibility that Jesus had actually come to Linda's bedroom. They recalled the words of Jesus recorded in the book Luke, chapter 10, verse 21; "I praise you, Father, Lord of heaven and earth, because you have hidden these things from the wise and learned, and revealed them to little children."

Linda's announcement combined with the scripture verse from Luke turned Mr. and Mrs. Amyx's concern for Linda's health into celebrated hope for a full recovery. It was enough to get them through what ended up being a very long rough patch. One year of bed rest turned into many. Linda Amyx, in fact, did not attend public school until seventh grade. Later, when asked how Linda's recovery was accomplished, Mrs. Amyx was quoted saying, "By faith in the Lord, long hours of prayer, an outstanding doctor and a cooperative patient."

For the Amyx family, Jesus wasn't a religious character from the Holy Bible made famous by Christians so he could act as a figurehead for hope and forgiveness. The Amyxs were devoted church people. But more importantly, they were genuine disciples of Christ. They loved the Lord and welcomed His presence in their home at every given opportunity. Linda was never afraid to say publicly, "Jesus is my best friend!"

The First Lady Sends Linda Get Well Wishes

A local reporter heard about Linda's plight. Without many friends or visitors to occupy her time, Linda was delighted to spend time with the journalist. He came to the house to get the full story. He took a photograph of Linda in bed next to her doll collection. Linda's Aunt Kay clipped the article with the photograph of her spunky niece and sent it to the First Lady of the United States, Mrs. Mamie Eisenhower. Shortly thereafter, a doll arrived from the White House. It was a Mamie doll, named after Mrs. Ike. With it came a long letter from the First Lady.

> *"Your Aunt, Mrs. Kenneth Burton, has sent me the picture and story about you which appeared in the newspaper recently. I was delighted to see such a lovely young lady and I must say that your smile is a very cheery one! You certainly have a wonderful collection of dolls to keep you company and I can well imagine how much fun you have with them. I am sure that you are doing everything Dr. Brown tells you to do and that before too long you will have completely recovered from your illness and will be able to run and play again. My very best wishes to you, Linda, for much happiness and a long life."*

> *Mamie Dowd Eisenhower*

Word about little Linda Amyx spread. She received letters from other well-known people such as Roy Rogers and his wife Cowgirl, Dale Evans. The youngster's network of well-wishers included celebrities, high-ranking politician's wives, neighbors, friends and, of course, her devoted family. Although her struggles were severe, she was cared for in a very loving environment. In fact, Linda was entirely shielded from destructive influences. Her confinement became an incubator for her favorite things.

Enchanted with American Indian Nations

Like other children growing up in the 1950's, Linda enjoyed playing with plastic toys and dolls. She read fascinating stories and countless books about Native American Indians. Smitten by descriptions of rustic landscapes and images of wild animals roaming free on the range, Linda became enamored with the southwest. She was very content with her collection of plastic toy horses, Native American dolls, a set of colored pencils and a box of crayons. She loved to draw animals, especially horses and sheep. She may not have realized it at the time, but her interest in Native American culture was developing into a passion, one that would eventually change her life.

Being a sickly child meant Linda had to give up or postpone certain hopes and dreams. Instead of becoming bitter because she couldn't go outside to play like other children, Linda found solace sketching and exchanging letters with pen pals. She eventually experienced the land, animals and people she had fallen in love with when her mother arranged a family vacation, a trip that allowed the Amyx family to travel and stay throughout the southwest. For Linda, the Indian Nations were all she had imagined them to be—and more.

Years later, in 1974, Linda decided to continue her infatuation with the southwest by seeking out a Navajo pen pal. She wanted to correspond with a Navajo woman, perhaps someone who loved wild horses as much as she did. The thing she didn't see coming was that she would fall hopelessly in love with a twenty-eight year-old prisoner at the Santa Fe state penitentiary, a Navajo man named Wilford Yazzie.

Without question, the most important factor that connected Linda to the love of her life was her illness. Her fragile state created a very unique situation—a cocoon-like childhood, which became the romantic foundation for things to come. Linda had faced and conquered extraordinary circumstances in her youth, so it should be no surprise to learn that later in life she faced and conquered other unforeseen circumstances, some of which would seem impossible to overcome.

CONFINEMENT

 *Linda*

*Trust in the Lord with all your heart, and lean not on your
own understanding; in all your ways acknowledge Him,
and He shall direct[a] your paths.*

Proverbs 3:5-6

"My name is Linda
and I am a Christian."

I was born into a very loving Christian home. I had an older
sister and two older brothers that spoiled me. Later, I got the baby
sister I always wanted. Our parents were extremely devoted when
it came to us children. We were a very close-knit family.

When I was four years old, I became very sick. My parents
were afraid I had the dreaded polio disease because I screamed in
pain every time anyone touched my legs. I couldn't even stand to
have the covers on them. After examining me, our beloved family
doctor told my anxious parents with tears in his eyes, "I wish it
was polio."

I had rheumatic fever, one of the feared illnesses of the 1950's caused by strep throat. At that time, complete bed rest was the cure-all for nearly every illness. Most of my childhood was spent alone in bed. My recovery was complicated because I also developed rheumatic heart disease. I was becoming weaker every day. Doctors didn't know how long I would last with my heart beating at such a high rate.

Our family physician had to prepare my parents for the worst. He told them that I might not be around in December, which is why they decided to celebrate Christmas in October that year. I knew nothing about my poor prognosis. The adults in my life spared me the anxiety of knowing how serious my condition was. Even though I was in such a weakened state, I enjoyed life. I loved my toy horses and dolls and would spend hours playing with them. I had a very vivid imagination.

One morning, Mom woke me up, and I told her that Jesus had come to see me during the night. She was used to my imaginary ramblings, so she said, "That's nice, dear." But I really got her attention when I told her, "Jesus picked me up and held me. He told me He wasn't going to take me to Heaven with Him just yet."

Mom fled the room in tears. She must have been crying because she knew God had answered our prayers for my recovery. We found out many people were praying because of the newspaper article that was published about me, "the smiling six-year old shut-in."

"Since You're Not Going To Live Long..."

For my schooling, I had a home tutor. The teacher was a retiree and perhaps a bit senile, which could explain why one day she told me, "Since you're not going to live long, I think I'll just let you draw and read as much as you like."

I never told my parents about her remarks until years later. I didn't want to upset them. As a result, I am the world's worst at math and science, but I still love to draw and read. I started public school in the seventh grade but was not allowed to take any gym, art or music classes. Doctor's orders stated that I was to avoid stairs, which meant I stayed on one floor as much as possible. This is the reason I had to eat lunch in a storeroom filled with textbooks. I still remember a teacher unlocking the door every day so I could go in and eat lunch. I didn't mind. Being alone in the storeroom gave me time to read my beloved books.

I was a teenager when my father passed away. After that, my older sister and her husband took my younger sister, our mother and me with them on vacation each year. I was able to visit the beautiful Southwest, the region of our country that I had imagined and read about for all those years. It was a dream come true when I finally got to meet a "real Indian."

Although my childhood wasn't normal by any means, it was a happy one. For me, normal was being surrounded by love and faith. I offically gave my heart to the Lord when I was eight years old, yet I don't remember a time when Jesus was not my best friend. I talked to Him as if He was sitting by my side, as indeed He was one night!

I'm Going to Be a Minister's Wife

I told Jesus I wanted to be a minister's wife and serve Him wherever He wanted to send me. I think this was because our minister and his wife (or Brother and Sister Patterson as they were called at Wesleyan Christian Church) had made such a deep impression on me as both ministers and friends of our family. I had no doubt that I would get well and fulfill all my dreams.

Even as a child, I believed in the power of prayer. I had no reason not to.

WHAT NOW

 *Jodie*

Who has woe? Who has sorrow? Who has contentions? Who has complaints? Who has wounds without cause? Who has redness of eyes? Those who linger long at the wine, those who go in search of mixed wine.

Proverbs 23:29–30

Getting expelled from Chilocco meant Wil had permanently ruined his chances of getting a high school diploma. Acquiring a General Education Diploma (GED), or a Good Enough Diploma, as some might say, was not on his list of things to do. Hanging around bars was inevitable. It was at some tavern he and a couple of bar flies got the idea that enlisting in the US Army would be the cool thing to do.

At the time, new recruits went straight to Vietnam after basic training, yet the idea of getting in shape and getting a regular paycheck trumped any cautionary thoughts of wartime danger. The U. S. government paid Army grunts more than any job on or near the reservation would pay. Wil and his friends didn't spend much time thinking about the actual consequences of fighting armed enemies in a war, or if they did, they weren't dissuaded.

Spared in War Only to Die a Senseless Death

When a friend of Wil's signed up for active duty at the Selective Service office in Farmington, Wil decided to do the same, but he had to go to Albuquerque to take the test and sign up. Wil was turned down because of his criminal record. As expected, after completing basic training, Wil's friend, Private Samuel Begay, went straight to Vietnam. He left the USA a proud United States soldier, but after taking a bullet to the head, he was sent home a disabled veteran. His injuries were severe enough to leave him with few choices for a vocation. Instead of life improving as he had hoped, everything got worse for Samuel. He found himself entrenched in old familiar ways—getting drunk and arrested.

One night Samuel woke up in the drunk tank with a half dozen, pain-in-the-neck, inebriated fools, which would have been all well and good if he had not had a seizure. It would have been better if he had been on the streets where fellow alcoholics would have taken care of him. But because he was in jail at the time, he had no hope of getting the medication that would have saved his life. His jailers had no sympathy. He was just another drunken Indian with the DTs[3]—or so they thought. Samuel was condemned to die a needless death in a drunk tank designed to keep drunken Indians off the streets and out of sight.

Many years later, when Wil learned of Samuel's death, he realized God had once again spared him from brutal destruction. If Wil had been allowed to enlist, he might have had a similar military experience. Like Samuel, Wil could have easily been

---

3 The DTs refer to delirium tremens, a symptom associated with alcohol withdrawal. In the U.S., fewer than fifty percent of alcoholics will develop any significant withdrawal symptoms upon cessation of alcohol intake, and, of these, only 5% of cases of acute ethanol withdrawal progress to delirium tremens. Unlike withdrawal syndrome associated with opiate dependence, DT (and alcohol withdrawal in general) can be fatal. Mortality was as high as 35% before the advent of intensive care and advanced pharmacotherapy.

sent to the front lines in the jungles of Vietnam. His friend's meaningless death disturbed Wil to the point he started to entertain ideas of how he might be able to help his people. He no longer envisioned himself an Olympic athlete or a heroic soldier, which gave him the freedom to try on a new dream.

Burdened with grief over the loss Samuel, Wil thought about what it would be like to be a social worker. The idea of helping fellow struggling Native Americans seemed like a noble pursuit. But instead of taking steps toward fulfilling that goal, he continued to drink excessively. Rather than helping, he remained part of the problem. And he had plenty of bad company to corrupt his good character.

The Booze Enthusiast's Merry-Go-Round

For Wil, having a couple sets of drinking buddies stashed around several states turned out to be a much needed resource—sort of like having a regional network of eager business associates at his disposal. Wil's buddies eventually found him floundering around in Oklahoma City and set him up with a job. At first, Wil felt lucky to be making butterscotch candies and suckers at the Bundy Candy Company. The job paid $1.25 an hour, $40 a week before taxes, which meant Wil took home a whopping $32.

Grabbing peanut butter candies for nourishment, Wil often stumbled into bed hungry. It wasn't long before he decided to quit his job at the candy company. Working in a factory for minimum wage was not his dream, nor was it anybody's dream job. It was what was available at the time.

Meanwhile, Wil's friends had scattered in different directions, none of which held much promise. Some went to the killing fields of Viet Nam, some went back to harsh reservation life and others became permanent residents of skid row in Oklahoma City or some place just like it. In reality, any metropolitan area where addicts could congregate with ease was embraced.

Wil had no resources with which to start a new life, not that having money tucked away would have changed anything. Money, whether earned or stolen, turned into booze, not rent. Occasionally, Wil dabbled in other ways of getting high, but alcohol was clearly his drug of choice. His addiction was becoming more and more visible, not that it mattered. At this point, no one cared who Wil Yazzie was, or what Wil Yazzie did.

For a number of years during his young adulthood, Wil was one of many Native American booze enthusiasts with nothing better to do than to camp out in front of or around a liquor store. He left the commercial premises only when temperatures dropped below freezing and he needed to find shelter. Alcoholics hanging around liquor stores were more like permanent fixtures, the kind nobody pays any attention to because they're always there. Although not a very welcoming image, liquor storeowners usually allowed loitering. Given that bank accounts benefited, the poisonous codependent situation was mostly overlooked.

At some point, Wil and a cousin dredged up enough ambition and made a trip to Colorado for work. His routine began by rising at 4:00 a.m. to make oatmeal and throw together a sack lunch so he could leave by 5:30 a.m. to begin his two-mile trek to work. It was mid December and bitter cold. Wil trudged through snow two feet deep in some parts, but instead of sticking to a job with potential, Wil went down another dead end path. The minute a paycheck arrived, any chance of a legitimate life evaporated.

Every bad decision Wil made turned into to a string of drunken episodes, and vice versa. Wil had no idea how little control he actually had, or what kind of merry-go-round he was on.

TRAPPED

Wil

*For I am persuaded that neither death nor life, nor angels
nor principalities nor powers, nor things present nor things
to come, nor height nor depth, nor any other created thing,
shall be able to separate us from the love of God which is in
Christ Jesus our Lord.*

Romans 8: 38-39

*"My name is Wil Yazzie
and I am a homeless alcoholic."*

I always thought I could stop drinking and reform on my
own. When I was a young man, I wanted to go to college and
make a life for myself. I did not understand how each time I took
up a bottle I was giving more and more of myself to Satan. I could
not see how drinking made everything in my life worse. Today,
I praise God that even on skid row He protected me. He loved and
cared for me when I was lost in my selfish ways. Without His
protection, I would be dead today and in hell in forever.

The Booze Enthusiast's Merry-Go-Round

I was trapped in a living hell in Oklahoma City. I was a hobo living on skid row. I never dreamed that I would sink to these depths. Because I was the only Navajo there, I was hated. I fought every day just to survive. I remember meeting a girl I knew from Chilocco. She invited me to a hotel where she and her brothers were staying. We got drunk but when they found out their new friend was a despised Navajo, they beat me and tried to throw me off the balcony. The girl managed to open the door for me so I could escape.

Once again, I found myself bruised and battered with no one to care for me. After that night, I wandered around Oklahoma City until I found some Navajo friends, maybe because I thought there would be safety in numbers. As Navajos, we united and went into seedy bars where we got into fights with other Natives from other tribes. We felt victorious even though nothing good ever came out of a bar fight.

I stayed in Oklahoma City for three years. My violent behavior had reached the point where there were times when no one wanted to be around me. One day, I was with some friends and we got into an argument. I took a knife from the kitchen and my friends got so frightened they took off. I looked around the apartment and found a wallet. Needless to say, I took the money someone had left behind. I bought a bus ticket and found my way back to Shiprock. But I didn't stay at home. I stayed with friends or slept on the ground. I had reached the point of no return. Alcohol plus anger was the perfect recipe for me to commit violence. It was a miracle that I did not kill someone during this time because I was full of both anger and alcohol.

Shortly after arriving in town, a couple friends and I got arrested for disorderly conduct and ended up in the Shiprock jail. We had been there for a couple days when one of the local Navajo ministers came to preach. If he had been white, I would have chased him out with my foul mouth. They didn't lock the door because of the minister being there, so after he left, we walked out. Once again, I was free—free from jail but not my addictions.

We knew the authorities were looking for us, so we hitched a ride to my dad's place in Newcomb, New Mexico. We stayed there one night. Then we hitched a ride to Window Rock, the capital of the Navajo Nation, where my older brother was working as an attorney for the DNA. The DNA is a branch of the Navajo government that provides legal aid to low income families. He already knew that we had escaped from jail. I told him we wanted to go to Phoenix so he gave me some money.

We spent a night in Winslow, Arizona on the way to Phoenix. Of course, we were drinking. After Winslow, we went to Flagstaff and caught a ride to Phoenix with a drunken Anglo man. He passed out so we took his whiskey and I continued to drive his car to Phoenix. We ended up in the skid row section of town. The man woke up angry so we just left him. To us, this was normal.

There were many Native Americans on skid row in Phoenix, which is why we felt right at home there. However, just as it was in Oklahoma City, there were a lot of fights between Navajos and other tribes. My days were spent fighting and drinking. When word spread that Navajos were the ones to attack, it became an all-out war on our tribe. My friends and I joined in on the fights. Then tragedy struck.

One of my friends was arrested for killing an African American man. Because we were together at the time, all three of us were arrested for homicide. Bruno and I didn't know that Daniel had killed a man. Thankfully, Daniel confessed to the police that we were not with him at the time of the murder. Bruno and I were released. Amazingly, we continued drinking and fighting. Looking back, it is hard to believe nothing scared us or caused us to want to change. The fact that Daniel had to serve two years of a five-year sentence for manslaughter in the Arizona State Penitentiary did not even shake me up.

I thought no one could stop me and I was in control. Even though I was a homeless alcoholic, I was arrogant. People were afraid of me. I think they thought I was crazy and would kill them. They were right. I was crazy. All sin is a form of insanity and my drunken rages had destroyed my sense of right and wrong.

I stayed drunk every day. It was as if I had a death wish. Even the threat of jail would not deter me from drinking. It seemed like I was in jail every other day. It got to the point where the staff at the Phoenix city jail knew me too well. I was recognized and accepted. "Hey, Roho. Welcome back!" The officers knew of my violent tendencies yet they still liked me for some reason. Looking back, I think being thrown in jail was actually the Lord putting me into His protective custody.

I didn't like the idea of going to prison, so one day when I was handcuffed to a string of other prisoners in a courtroom awaiting trial, I managed to slip out of my handcuffs. When the opportunity presented itself, I jumped through a glass door and ran toward freedom. One of the officers tried to grab me and was cut by the broken glass in the struggle but that didn't stop me. A bunch of officers chased me down the street.

Freedom lasted for four blocks. I was apprehended by a patrol car and taken back to jail where they stripped me and put me into solitary confinement. For about a week, I slept on the cold cement floor and drank from the toilet bowl. It was a miserable low point—even for me.

At my next court appearance, I was not only handcuffed but my feet were also shackled. Two officers of the law accompanied me. I was sentenced to eight months in the Phoenix city jail, which I thought was unbelievably lenient. I could have been given a much harsher sentence and sent to the state prison for assaulting an officer during my attempted escape from the courtroom.

After my release, I returned to skid row and drinking. As the proverb says, I was like a dog returning to its vomit. I was the fool who keeps repeating his folly. A drinking buddy found me in a bar one night and suggested we head out to Flagstaff, Arizona. Almost as soon as we arrived we lost each other because of being so drunk. I stayed in Flagstaff for a week and then hitchhiked to Farmington, New Mexico. I was about to enter a new chapter in my life, this time as a gang leader. One of only two significant towns in San Juan County, Farmington was about to become Roho territory. Although a life of crime often makes good reading material, it is never good. In my case, nothing good happened when I was drinking.

FUGITIVE WANTED

 *Jodie*

Revive me, O Lord, for Your name's sake! For Your righteousness' sake bring my soul out of trouble.

Psalm 143:11

Unfortunately, sober relatives, citizens or police officers are the ones who have to deal the filth and chaos alcoholics create and leave behind—and it's never pleasant.

During the years Wil was drinking and living on the streets in San Juan and/or McKinley counties, a protective custody program was in place, which meant Wil and his drinking buddies were back on the streets by nightfall after spending twelve hours (or so) behind bars in a disgusting "drunk tank." The mixture of addiction and aimlessness kept Wil and his friends hopelessly trapped in a merry-go-around lifestyle of misdeeds and misfortune. Without incentives or resources to break the cycle, chronic drinking turned into a perpetual problem.

Drinking Toilet Water in a Prison Cell

Wil ended the '60s in a courtroom chained to a dozen or more criminals where he managed to slip out of his handcuffs. Then, when the opportunity presented itself, he fled the courtroom by kicking then jumping through a glass door. Turning himself into a very wanted fugitive and successfully adding another misdemeanor felony charge to his growing rap sheet was merely another episode in the misadventures of Wil Yazzie—the low point of which would be flushing the prison toilet and drinking incoming fresh water to quench his thirst and prevent dehydration.

This incident alone should have been enough to deter Wil from future self-destructive behavior, but it wasn't. Things got deceptively better when five months into his sentence he was released. Wil may have been given an early release from prison but he certainly was not finished with drinking.

Saved by Tuberculosis

Predictably, Wil met up with his drinking buddies and ended up on skid row in Farmington. Sharing booze meant drinking from a common bottle, which is how Wil ended up with tuberculosis. Thankfully, public health officials properly diagnosed his condition, took him off the streets and placed him in a sanitarium. After six months of medication and proper nutrition, he was declared disease-free and healthy, though he was far from it.

After his release, he bounced back and forth from Phoenix to Farmington, not caring about anyone or anything other than "finding some drink." Sadly, Wil knew firsthand how alcohol poisoning unexpectedly extinguishes human life. He had witnessed numerous friends suffer through ugly convulsions as they turned blue only to be revived by emergency crews in the nick of time. And yet, he did not consider quitting until the unthinkable happened and he experienced his worst nightmare—his first alcoholic seizure.

As terrifying as hallucinations of hissing snakes and

menacing spiders were, they did not traumatize him like the thought of experiencing the DTs (delirium tremens). Hallucinations were a sure indicator that the DTs were coming his way, yet Wil did nothing to avoid the inevitable. He was deceived into thinking that he could control how his body reacted to overdoses of alcohol. He told himself, *that'll never happen to me.* Wil was wrong.

It happened at night, but instead of being alone out on the street where medical help would have been too late, Wil was in the safe confines of a drunk tank. Sick with a malicious hangover, Roho started to shake badly. After a shower, the uncontrollable shaking got worse. He called for help. Scared to lie down, his only hope was to call a friend to bail him out so he could re-up his alcohol intake. His last recollection was signing his name to make a phone call and then being put into an ambulance. The fact that Wil did not succumb to alcohol poisoning that night had to be yet another act of divine protection.

We Drink Anything, Including Lysol

With the help of experienced hospital personnel, Wil got through his first case of the DTs and then promptly ignored their advice. He did not go to rehab. He didn't even consider it. Instead, the first thing he did upon his release from the hospital was to nurse his addiction with some booze. Outside the hospital door stood one of Wil's eager associates, a cohort armed with the alcoholic's sure-fire prescription for the DTs, something 80, or better yet, 100-proof. Alcoholics are not above drinking shoe polish, Lysol, Listerine, aftershave, or anything else with alcohol in it.

Once again, Wil managed to cheat death. If he had died from either his battle with tuberculosis or complications stemming from the DT's, medical personnel could have easily connected the dots and declared his death alcohol-related. And they would have been correct.

ARRESTED AGAIN

 *Wil*

You shall have no other gods before Me.

Exodus 20:3

"My name is Roho.
I am my own god."

In 1969, the city of Farmington, New Mexico became my world. Some childhood friends from Shiprock introduced me to a gang called the Renegades. There were about three hundred gang members in Farmington and all of them were involved in drugs and stealing. Some members I knew specialized in bootlegging liquor. At that time, alcohol was not sold on Sundays, so bootleggers sold cheap wine at high prices to alcoholics who could not miss a day without liquor. This was how the Renegades supported their lifestyle.

After my introduction to the Renegades, access to drugs and alcohol became easier. For me, it was a perfect fit. Some gang members would go home to "dry out" for a while but would come back with money, so partying became an endless cycle for those of us who stayed on the streets. I did not go back home to Shiprock. Instead, I lived on the streets of Farmington. Unless I was in jail for disorderly conduct or public drunkenness, I was drinking every single day.

It Won't Happen To Me

During my time with the Renegades, I had seen approximately twenty people die. They were not old "winos" as some would suppose. Most were in their late teens and early twenties, and they all died from alcohol-related incidents or suicide. One friend died in my arms. He died of an alcohol-related seizure. We were in jail at the time. I tried to revive him, but the jailers didn't care. He was just another Indian who had drunk himself to death.

Like all young people, we never thought anything life threatening would happen to us, but Satan is always looking for victims. He knows that if a young person will believe his "it won't happen to me" lie, he has found a potential candidate for hell. I was one of those people. I had become my own god. I thought Roho was invincible.

Next to drinking, I loved to fight. Sometimes we would get drunk and fistfight among ourselves. The Renegades were all Navajos so we would fight other tribes who dared to come to our "turf." Anglos were afraid of us so they never came to our area of town. We were in total control—or so we thought.

God Sends an Angel

Something happened during this period of my life that made me think God was protecting me and perhaps trying to interrupt my self-destructive behavior. I was staying at my cousin's home and returned there one day after work. No one was home, so I decided to lie down and rest for a while. I was tired. I remember hoping my cousins had gone to buy some liquor.

I was dozing when I felt someone stroking my hair. I looked up and a woman was holding my head in her lap. I was unable to see her face because her hair was very long and fell around her face. I asked her who she was but received no answer. To this day I do not understand how she got up and put my head back on the pillow. As she was leaving, I could see in the half-light that she was dressed in traditional clothing. She left the room without opening the door. She went through through the door. I opened the door and ran after her—I had to know who she was. But I could not find her anywhere. She had disappeared even though it was impossible for her to get away so quickly.

Even though I was a superstitious Navajo at the time, I was not afraid of this mysterious woman. It was a good feeling to experience the love that emanated from her. Knowing what I know now, I believe she was sent by God to tell me that I was loved and to prepare me for the difficult days ahead.

Arrested For Something I Did Not Do

Although I deserved to be arrested for many things, I was arrested in 1971 for something I didn't do. It was Christmas day and a bootlegger friend asked me to help him burglarize a store. I refused to do it, but Stanley kept insisting. He wanted to commit a crime in broad daylight. To shut him up, I agreed to go along. I wanted to see just how easy his "easy target" was. After seeing the store, I told him it would be foolish to break such a big window to steal a few items, so I left. I was two blocks away when I heard the window shatter.

I returned to my cousin's place. Later that afternoon, Stanley showed up with the news that someone had seen and recognized him. I told him he should go back to Shiprock, but before he fled, he told me he had several radios stashed in a nearby dumpster. That same evening another friend and I found the stolen radios and stashed them at a Renegade hide-out called the mudhut. The mudhut stood next to a couple abandoned railroad boxcars in a heavily weeded area. A couple days later, I went back and took two of the radios to my cousin's apartment where I hid them in the ceiling.

Two weeks passed and nothing happened. Then some friends wanted to borrow some money from me. I told them I didn't have any cash but I knew where two hot radios were stashed. I got them from their hiding place, put them in a paper bag and gave the radios to my friends with instructions not to tell anyone that they had gotten them from me.

Of course the police stopped them. And of course they told the police I had given them the radios, but not before adding, "We had had no idea the radios were stolen!" That afternoon a detective came to my cousin's apartment and took me in for questioning. However, when we arrived at police headquarters, I was not asked about stolen radios. I was questioned about a murder instead.

The murder victim was a man who had been brutally beaten and later crashed at my cousin's apartment. I identified him as the man I couldn't get to wake up the morning after he showed up. I told the police we called 911 for an ambulance and he was taken to the hospital where he later died. Satisfied I was telling the truth, I was released. I returned to my cousin's apartment.

Since there was no mention made about stolen radios, I thought I was in the clear. But later that night, a police officer came to the apartment with a warrant for my arrest. Supposedly, I had admitted I was the lookout during the burglary, yet I had never given such a testimony about the break-in or anything else.

When I read the statement, I noticed the charge was "accessory to burglary" and that someone had forged my signature. At the time, Farmington was a very racist town, so it could have been the police, or it could have been Stanley. He might have been told he would get a lighter sentence by involving me. If it was Stanley, it didn't help him. He was sent to the state penitentiary in Santa Fe, New Mexico. Whoever it was, I owe them my life. I'm alive today because of the time I spent in prison.

I was taken to the Aztec County jail where I remained for two months. Each Sunday, a preacher from a local church would come hold services for the inmates. I was so angry and full of hate for the "white man's religion" and so crazed by my desire for alcohol, that I hurled obscenities and cups of water at them as they spoke. I was like a wild animal. By the end of my sixty-day incarceration, I was desperate for a drink. When my attorney told me to plead guilty so I could get out that day, I immediately agreed.

Prisoner # 9326

I was taken to the judge's office where I was sentenced to three years probation. I should have been charged with a misdemeanor—for receiving stolen property valued under $100.00. But the forged signature document bumped the "accessory to a burglary" misdemeanor charge up to a felony. Stanley could have been brought in to testify on my behalf, but my attorney told the judge Stanley could not be located even though they knew he was in the Santa Fe prison. Nobody wanted to help me. After all, I had a reputation—I was a worthless, no good troublemaker.

After my release, I went straight back to Farmington and got drunk. I thought I had beat the system by pleading guilty. But in reality, I had set myself up to go to prison. During this time, my probation officer had overlooked many of my violations, most of which involved public drunkenness. Then one day, eleven months later, he put out a warrant for my arrest. In late 1972, I was arrested and sent to the state penitentiary in Santa Fe, New Mexico.

Doing time in a local jail or drunk tank is easier than doing time in a state penitentiary. Prison life is much more challenging and coldhearted. Prison not only takes away your freedom but it also tries to strip away your identity. I had turned into a number. When I heard "Yazzie, 9326," I went wherever and did whatever I was told. I should have been frightened in prison, but I wasn't. I already knew how to survive all kinds of violence. I considered myself tough enough to endure anything. My heart was hardened and no one could break Roho.

Chapter Fifteen

IT SEEMED RIGHT AT THE TIME

There is a way that seems right to a man, ut its end is the way of death.

Proverbs 14: 12

*"My name is Wil Yazzie
and I am a convicted felon."*

After four months at the state prison, I was sent to the Los Lunas Correctional Facility in Central New Mexico. They had an honor farm at Los Lunas where prisoners were allowed to irrigate fields, bundle hay and do whatever else needed to get done. At the time, Los Lunas was part of New Mexico's prison trusty system. To my amazement, I was considered a "trustee"—a prisoner who could be trusted to work (and not escape). Then, after only three months, I was paroled.

The parole board arranged for Robert and Ann Parks to pick me up in Farmington. They were a nice Anglo couple who worked with Native American alcoholics. I don't know why they had faith in me, but they did. They were the first people who saw me not as a hopeless sinner but as the man I could become through Jesus Christ. They picked me up in June 1973 and I lived with them in Farmington for about a week.

Despite Robert and Ann's prayers to the contrary, I returned to drinking and violated my parole. I was sent back to Santa Fe and remained there for three months before returning to Los Lunas. Again, I worked the fields. Since I had grown up working on a farm, working outside was not hard for me.

Security was very lax on the honor farm. There were no fences or guard towers. A fellow trustee decided to make a run for liquor after roll call that night and I was only too happy to go with him. We didn't make it back before the next roll call. They caught us, which meant we were going to be taken to the Valencia County Jail. We didn't want to go to jail so we decided to escape. At the time, it seemed like the right thing to do.

On A Horse Named Happy

We took a horse from Los Lunas named Happy and rode him to the liquor store. Once we arrived, we released him to go back to the farm, but first we threw his bridle into a nearby stream. Again, at the time, it seemed like the right thing to do.

We tried to steal a car but were unable to hotwire it. Not wanting to leave empty handed, we stole beer instead. We met up with some Native people from the Isleta Reservation. They didn't know who we were or that we had escaped from Los Lunas. As far as they were concerned, we were their new drinking buddies. They agreed to take us back to their reservation where we partied and got drunk.

As usual, I found myself involved in a drunken brawl. This time it was with my fellow escapee. I passed out in an alfalfa field. When I woke up the next morning, I was alone.

From there I hitched a ride to Albuquerque, and while talking to someone there, I saw my escapee buddy. He said he knew a family in Albuquerque so I joined him and went to their home. We stayed there for a couple days and then decided to hitchhike our way to Farmington.

Hiding Escaped Prisoners

An elderly Mexican couple picked us up in a small town called Cuba. We rode in the back of their pickup where they had a refrigerator covered with a heavy canvas tarp. Outside of Cuba, police motioned the couple to pull over. It was a roadblock. The police were looking for some escaped prisoners—us! We were hiding under the tarp and thought we had reached the end of our adventure. I suppose because our accomplices were so old, the police officers assumed they wouldn't be the type to help escaped prisoners. The police told the old couple to go on.

As it turned out, two other inmates had escaped from the honor farm after we did. They hitched a ride on a freight train to Gallup and beat us to Farmington. We eventually met up at a bar, and while we were heavily intoxicated, we decided to break into the office of a secluded car lot. All of us grabbed car keys off the wall. One of my keys started a car, so we drove off in that car. We were onto our next adventure. Once again, it seemed like the thing to do.

We siphoned gas from a parked car, stole some tools and decided to go see my dad in Newcomb, New Mexico. I told my dad that I had been paroled. Although I'm not sure he believed me, he loaded us up with food anyway. It could have been that he felt sorry for his loser son. We headed to Gallup where we sold the tools to buy more liquor. That same evening, I drove to Kayenta, Arizona in a blackout. I shudder when I think of how many lives I have endangered by driving in alcoholic blackouts. It was only by the grace of God that I wasn't killed or that innocent people weren't killed by me.

Somehow we made it to my escapee partner's home in

Kayenta. When we were getting ready leave, my partner told us his brother wanted to come along, so with one more added to the gang, we all took off. We noticed a truck parked on the side of the road and stopped out of curiosity. There were two cowboys in the truck. They were passed out and they had a full case of beer, so we decided to help ourselves. Unfortunately, they woke up, which started a fight.

Indians Fighting Cowboys for a Case of Budweiser

All of a sudden, while I was still taking and giving punches, my two buddies jumped in our car and took off, leaving me behind with two angry cowboys. I didn't like my odds, so I ran after my friends. They saw me running and stopped for me. We escaped the cowboys and made it to Shiprock that night. Even though we were fighting horrible hangovers the next morning, we got back in our stolen car and went on the hunt for more booze.

On our way to Farmington, the car broke down in small town called Waterflow. With one guy passed out, my escapee partner and his brother decided they would get their revenge for when I started a fight on the Isleta Reservation. Just as they jumped me, some Shiprock friends passed by and came to my rescue. When the odds changed to favor us, the fight ended quickly.

I couldn't wake up my passed out buddy, so I left him behind and decided to keep moving. Another friend from Hogback drove by and offered to take me to Farmington. Even though I did not really care whose car he was driving, I asked him anyway. He pointed to the man passed out on the passenger side and said, "Him." We drove to a dirt road and pushed the intoxicated owner of the car out and continued onto Farmington. Now I wonder, who would do this kind of thing? We had to be completely out of our minds.

Don't Move or I'll Blow Your Head Off

We were traveling east on Route 64 when the state police

stopped us in Fruitland. They had pulled us over for a missing taillight, but the police officer recognized me. He knew I was one of the escapees from Los Lunas. He quickly pulled out his gun and held it to my head. "Don't move, or I'll blow your head off!" I was handcuffed, put into his patrol car and taken to the Aztec County jail for the night.

The next day I asked the jailor if I could make a phone call. He and I were friends, so he took me out of my cell, dialed the number for me and left me there—by myself. There were a lot of trustees hanging around so I just walked out the door. One of the trustees followed me and the two of us just kept walking. We had gone about a mile and a half when I decided to go back. I thought, "Why am I running? They'll eventually find me no matter where I go."

I was tired of running and ready to surrender. When we reached the top of a hill, we saw a half a dozen officers of the law and a police dog. They were searching for us so I shouted, "Up here!" Using a bullhorn, they told us to lay on the ground with our hands behind our backs, and that's what I did.

After that, I was put into solitary at the Aztec Jail. Someone finally took my running skills seriously. By this time, I had become quite the escape artist.

COSTLY MISTAKES

 *Jodie*

Beware lest anyone cheat you through philosophy and empty deceit, according to the tradition of men, according to the basic principles of the world, and not according to Christ.

Colossians 2:8

In or out of jail, on or off the reservation, Wil had no hope of real recovery or a life with meaning. His human relationships were based on cravings and an unhealthy infatuation with passing out. When your jailers have become friendly acquaintances, something has gone awry. Familiarity with prison guards wasn't what Wil needed. What Wil needed he never got.

Wil's well-meaning relatives introduced him to things during his childhood that would continue to haunt him well into his adulthood. Not only was he initiated into the very real, supernatural spirit world through traditional medicine man ways, but he was also introduced to the world of gambling through what must have looked like innocent games. The Navajo shoe game brought Wil and his elders together on a regular basis. Wil was like every other kid who craved attention; he liked spending time with the adults in his life.

Gambling in the Desert

Playing betting games and learning the ways of the medicine man were important elements of Wil's heritage as a young Navajo. As a result, a significant part of Wil's childhood was spent gambling in the desert. The gaming inspired fellowship that often lasted until 4 a.m. in the morning. Clan against clan, betting sheep against sheep, elders betting their boy would be the one who would find the Tsá'ászi'ts'óóz (narrowleaf yucca) from a buried shoe—this was Navajo playtime.

However, some of what Wil absorbed from his relatives did more harm than good. First, a gambling addiction took root in Wil. It would take decades before Wil could admit gaming was a costly habit.

Skinwalkers

Superstitious beliefs left little room for other beliefs, especially those that dismissed certain aspects of the Navajo way of life. For many Native Americans, Biblical Christianity was considered to be a conflicting belief system, one that appeared eager to replace an honorable culture.

Superstitions are widespread within Native American communities. Once reaching momentum, myths tend to take on a life of their own and can easily get out of control. For example, skinwalkers are something to be feared. In the Navajo language, they are called Yee Naaldlooshii, which translates to "[beings] that travel on four legs." Although many Navajo families maintain their own stories about skinwalkers, they are never encouraged to share them. It's taboo to talk about "witches" in polite company. There's a troublesome notion that a skinwalker might be listening and get even with you by causing you harm.

Young Wil was familiar with skinwalkers. As far as he was concerned, they were able to run long distances and had supernatural abilities enabling them to fly across canyons and run as fast as cars. Skinwalkers were "known" to attack vehicles and cause car accidents. None of this fazed brave Wil Yazzie. He had no reason to be concerned until he, along with two cousins and a friend, had a little midnight game of hide 'n seek with a mischievous skinwalker.

The teenagers were returning home following an evening of Keshjee', the traditional Navajo shoe game when out in the middle of nowhere, something (or someone) appeared. "Did you see that?" they asked one another.

The girl did not see the shadowy figure standing by the side of the road but all three boys did. Wil and his two cousins witnessed and described the same thing and each account was identical. The body and face were completely white, but from the waist down, the figure was covered with animal fur.

Wil remembers the incident vividly. "He had long hair and wore a lot of turquoise jewelry," Wil says matter-of-factly recalling the strange sighting. "We were frightened, yet we backed up the car to look for him. He was gone. He had been standing by the edge of a sixty or seventy-foot cliff. Beyond that, there was a river so it was not possible for him to disappear like he did."

Many years later, Wil found out both boys who were with him that night had died. One lost his life in a horrible car wreck and the other died in a prison fight. Wil began thinking it was the skinwalker's witchcraft that had caused the fatalities. Naturally, Wil thought he was on the hit list. Two out of three witnesses were dead; only one remained. Yet, dozens of car wrecks and near death experiences later, Wil lives.

It would be impossible to count the actual number of times Wil has escaped death. Satan's attempts to extinguish him started when he was very young, but Wil knows now with absolute certainty that God protected him throughout the years. And when the Creator has a plan for your life, no hairy half-man, half-animal can triumph over the Almighty.

Wil did not have solid scriptural teaching to correct his superstitious tendencies, some of which had opened the door to demonic influences. Finding acceptance in all the wrong places, that was Wil's specialty, and that is how Drinking Buddies, Spirits in the Night and Fellow Ex-Convicts became his clan folk.

With several warrants out for his arrest, Wil took up running, not for trophies like in high school but to avoid lawmen who knew him by mug shot and name. Hitching rides, jumping on trains, joining other escapees, life on the run was risky, especially since Wil had taken up smoking pot and using pills to get high. His situation was escalating, as was his behavior. He sold drugs to addicts and girls for sex; he did whatever it took to bring in money.

Feeding Addictions

To make sure his addictions got fed, Wil found it easy to engage in an assortment of illegal acts. However, breaking into a car lot and stealing a vehicle then drinking and driving the stolen car while state troopers and local police have you on their most wanted list turned out to be a significant lapse in judgment. No one, least of all prison escapees, should make significant decisions while they are alcohol-impaired. Yet, it would be decades before Wil Yazzie would acknowledge this truth.

Wil's bad decisions often impaired his freedom. One foolish thing led to another and the chain reaction usually ended with Wil behind bars. Stealing beer from cowboys was one of those mistakes Wil and his friends made after they went AWOL, leaving the Los Lunas Correctional Facility without permission. For two cowboys with XXL-sized physiques and attitudes, it was no big deal to reprimand a couple of drunken Indians. Alcohol had triggered another frivolous cycle of breaking the law, drunken arguing and reckless driving.

Driving through the Navajo Nation involves extremely long stretches of deserted roadways. Few cars travel through the desolate reservation wilderness at night. Because of this, impaired drivers only have to concentrate on avoiding other drivers once every half hour or so. In Wil's case, this worked to his advantage until Wil's post cowboy joyride back to Farmington was cut short by flashing red and blue lights. A state police officer stopped the car prepared to give someone a ticket for a missing taillight. The officer did not seem to care about the stolen car, or that Wil and his buddies were drinking. He did, however, become energized when he recognized his traffic stop had produced wanted fugitives—Wilford Yazzie being the top priority.

Freedom Never Lasts Long

The bunch of them were taken to Aztec City Jail, a place Wil had checked into so many times he should have been awarded some kind of ACJ frequent offender miles. At the very least, his photo should have been plastered on a cell wall somewhere. When his turn came up to make his one phone call, Wil decided he would rather not go to jail. Because the jailer knew Wil (like a flight attendant knows his or her frequent flyers) his guard was down. Wil took advantage of the familiar relationship and snuck out the back door of the jail's kitchen.

Freedom didn't last long. He was apprehended at the top of a nearby mesa.

"Hands behind your head!" Wil knew the drill.

A week later, he left Aztec City Jail to begin his prison sentence at the Santa Fe State Penitentiary. The authorities were aggravated and Wil was the primary reason for their indignation. Shortly after switching prison uniforms, Wil ended up in solitary confinement for his numerous attempts to escape incarceration. Solitary confinement was exactly where the Lord wanted Wil—alone and sober in a barely habitable space.

PEN PALS

 *Linda*

Remember the prisoners as if chained with them—those who are mistreated—since you yourselves are in the body also.

Hebrews 13:3

*"My name is Linda
and I am an evangelical Christian."*

People have often asked me, "How naïve were you that you would write a prisoner you had never met?"

The truth is no one who asked me that question had any idea of just how innocent, naïve and trusting I was. Given that I did not go to school and was not around other children, I welcomed the opportunity to write and receive letters. This why I became so fond of pen pals. Even in middle school and high school when I attended school regularly, I couldn't participate in any activities. I had to rest after school each day, so my pen pals continued to be my primary friends.

When I was in high school I started writing to a girl who lived in England and another girl from Los Angeles. Janet was my British pen pal and Judi was my West Coast pen pal. We were all Sonny and Cher fans. To this day, the three of us still stay in touch with each other. I've had the pleasure of meeting both of my pen pals. Janet came to visit me in Ohio once. She was one of the sweetest women anyone could ever hope to meet. Judi and I met when my family went to Disneyland for a vacation in 1968. True fans that we were, we went to the Hollywood Wax Museum and had our photos taken in front of the Sonny and Cher wax figures.

Classified Ad in the Navajo Times

A few years later, in September 1974 when I was twenty-six years old, I placed a classified ad in the Navajo Times requesting a Navajo pen pal. Much to my surprise, I received about fifty letters from Navajo men. I had never been on a date in my life so I wasn't expecting letters from MEN! In many ways, I was still a child even though I was twenty-six years old. I had no idea about evil in the world. To say I trusted people would be an understatement.

One response came from a male Navajo prisoner in Texas. He sounded despondent in his "I saw your classified ad in the Navajo Times" introduction letter, so I wrote him back and told him about my Christian beliefs. In his next letter, he told me I was the only truly "straight" person he had ever "met."

I also got a letter from a Navajo man in San Quentin Prison who was getting out in a couple months. He wanted someone to write to for a short while. He thought exchanging letters would make time go faster. I answered his letter as well as others, thanking everyone for writing. I had to tell them that I had received too many letters to correspond with them all. Oddly enough, only a few letters were strange, and those letters did not come from prisoners.

The truth was only one letter stood out for me. It was a letter from Wilford Yazzie, prisoner #23126 from the Santa Fe Penitentiary. I felt a bond with him right from the start. Now

I realize that it was Lord who put Wil in my life. After reading his letter, I had no interest in any of the other letters.

I thought it was strange that I didn't receive any letters from Navajo women, which is what I really wanted. I was shy and didn't want to write to men. After all, what would I say to them? I wasn't interested in dating. I honestly didn't think I would ever marry unless it was to a pastor or a ministerial student. I had decided I would be a pastor's wife, or no wife at all.

Kindred Spirits

Wil was special to me from the very beginning. We never lacked anything to talk about. I wrote to him every day and felt I could tell him anything. It may sound strange, but I was convinced I had found a kindred spirit in Wil even though there couldn't be two people more opposite. For some people, there is only one special mate. For me, that special someone is Wil Yazzie.

My mom was not pleased that I was writing a man in prison. She knew the full extent of my innocence so she was right to worry about me. She knew I was extremely tenderhearted and compassionate. I was (still am) the kind of person who would dissolve into tears while reading a sad book or watching a sad movie.

I had always been a very obedient daughter, but when it came to corresponding with Wil, I felt I was right. I did not see Wil as a criminal. To me, he was just someone who needed the Lord. I saw him not as he was but as what he could be. From the very first letter, I had a sense that God had His hand upon Wil and He had a purpose for his life. I even dreamed that one day he would become a minister. I imagined his testimony would be tremendous and have a great effect on others.

In Love with a Prison Pen Pal

During the time he and I exchanged letters, he shared intimate things with me that he had probably never shared with anybody else. I was chatty but also evangelistic. I talked about our family pets, my parents and siblings, our church life, and of course, the Lord and what He was doing in my life. I told him how when I was eight years old I gave my heart to the Lord at local revival meeting. I included how the minister was in his eighties and that by the second night I wanted to cleanse my soul by confession. I couldn't wait for the altar call. Of course, I prayed for Wil's salvation and encouraged him to go to church whenever he could while he was in prison. Wil was receptive.

By Valentine's Day 1975, I was in love. Even though my soul mate lived 1400 miles away and was incarcerated, I began to think my dreams of being a minister's wife would be fulfilled.

Chapter Eighteen

NOTHING TO LOSE

 *Wil*

Do not be deceived, God is not mocked; for whatever a man sows, that he will also reap.

Galatians 6:7

*"My name is Prisoner #23126
and I am a deceiver."*

Solitary confinement was the lowest point of my life up to that time. I did not like being alone in a dark cell in the Santa Fe Penitentiary. One of my fellow Renegades was a prison trustee and allowed to clean the walkway. When I got the chance, I asked him to get me something to read. He found some old magazines and a copy of the Navajo Times newspaper for me. I glanced through the newspaper and saw a classified ad from a woman in Cincinnati, Ohio. She was looking for a Navajo pen pal. I couldn't respond because I was in confinement, but I put the newspaper away where I could get to it later.

I was released from my dungeon after a week. Prison guards

escorted me back into "population." In other words, I went back to dormitory style cells where I was housed with other inmates. I knew I was going to spend years in prison, so I decided to write the woman from Ohio. I had nothing but time on my hands, and I had nothing to gain or lose. I didn't expect to receive an answer. I had a bad temper and my heart was stubborn, so I didn't care if I did or didn't hear back from the pen pal seeking woman.

I received a letter from Linda Amyx. It felt so good to get a letter in prison. Soon we were writing to each other every day. Linda's letters gave me something to look forward to each day. At mail call, the other inmates began to notice me. I was getting letters at least twice a week. They would mock, "Yazzie, he'll get a letter. He always gets a letter."

Linda's Belief in Me

I didn't think our friendship would last long. I was used to people giving up on me. All my so-called friends from Farmington had abandoned me. But Linda was different. She was not like anyone I had ever known. I could tell by her letters that she was innocent and trusting. For the first time in my life, someone loved me for me. Linda actually believed in me.

One would think that with daily letters Linda and I would soon run out of things to say, but that didn't happen. We talked about everything and shared confidences with one another. I usually talked about myself or about what was happening on the outside in the free world. Linda shared with me about Jesus Christ and I became interested. I started going to church services. I also joined some Bible studies and started to believe in myself. My attitude and outlook was slowing shifting.

After several months in Santa Fe, I went before the judge at the Valencia County courthouse. I was facing more charges involving evading the police. I received another one to five year sentence and a new number, #24486. At this point, I had two numbers and nothing to look forward to except more time in prison, so I got my GED and took the ACT college entrance exams.

I enrolled in the College of Santa Fe and took classes held inside the prison. Life was changing for me. I was in love, and for the first time in a long time, I sensed that I had uncovered a purpose for my life. It was a new feeling.

Developing A Burden For Others

I wanted to become a social worker because of what I had seen going on in prison. I saw young people who came to prison thinking they could do what they did in the free world. But prison life has its own unique culture. In prison, there is physical violence and sexual abuse to combat, sometimes on a daily basis. After meeting Linda and hearing about Jesus Christ, my heart began to soften. I developed a burden for others. I had always cared for others, but this new feeling of sympathy and concern was different. I actually wanted to help young people so that they would never come to this hellish place.

Even though I believed in Jesus Christ and attended services at the prison chapel, I had not completely surrendered my life to the Lord. Satan still had his grip on my life. I was addicted to gambling, which was a favorite pastime in prison. Drugs were also readily available. I wanted to surrender to God's plan for my life, but I thought if I truly gave my heart to the Lord, I would have to become gentle and meek like Him. And in prison, one has to always be ready to resist and fight or be killed.

Linda sent me money every week. She naively believed that I was using it to buy snacks in the canteen. Actually, I was using it to feed my addictions. I used her money to gamble and then used my earnings for snacks. That was how I rationalized my behavior. I convinced myself I wasn't deceiving Linda.

I truly loved Linda. I was under the impression that an education and a belief in Jesus would help me change on my own. I wanted to be the man she thought I was. In reality, no amount of education or self-will can change a person's heart. Only Jesus Christ can change a person's heart.

Chapter Nineteen

DANGEROUS BUT SACRED GROUND

Jodie

But the fruit of the Spirit is love, joy, peace, longsuffering, kindness, goodness, faithfulness, gentleness, self-control. Against such there is no law.

Galatians 5:22-23

Without ever dating, Wil and Linda fell in love.

Let's be honest. An inmate who starts out a pen pal and ends up a husband—there's a lot that could go wrong in that situation. Strangers who become lovers because they bared their souls to one another in a string of me-then-you, you-then-me chain letters... come on! It's completely romantic, or it's a scam. The notion of falling in love through letter writing is somewhat sketchy territory, but in Wil and Linda's case, it turned out to be sacred territory.

Attention-grabbing stories of prison marriages usually end with heartache and disappointment, not happily-ever-after. That's not to say Linda and Wil skipped heartache and disappointment. On the contrary. However, a single classified ad placed at the right time in the right place and read by the right person created a truly extraordinary marriage.

> FEBRUARY 1974. "I would like to exchange letters with a Navajo pen pal. My family (my mother, my two sisters and a brother-in-law and I) just returned from a vacation where we very much enjoyed being on the Navajo Reservation and with Navajo people. We especially enjoyed going to a rodeo in Kayenta, Arizona. I'm 26 years old. God bless, Linda, Lockland, Ohio."

The ad received numerous responses, which, for the optimistic librarian's assistant, was remarkable and slightly daunting. She answered a handful of the letters but only one stood out from the reply pile. For some reason, only Wil Yazzie's letter made an impression on her.

Opposites Attract

Two weeks after responding to her ad, Wil received his first letter from Linda. She was a devoted Christian. He was a hardened criminal. An unexpected friendship quickly turned into romance. If Linda were reaching out in the same fashion today, she might have had a hard time finding her soul mate. Although con artists have always been around, malicious internet and prison pen pal frauds have clearly changed the quixotic milieu where Wil and Linda found each other. Even in 1974, Linda was treading in dangerous waters.

Apart from Wil's criminal background and closeted addictions, everything between Wil and Linda was pure and innocent. In what at first appeared to be just a casual, voyeuristic peek into another person's life, these two completely opposite individuals found unexpected tenderness, vulnerability and true love.

LINDA: I think about you all the time!!! I can't believe you're real!

WIL: Thank you for the way you know me. Thank you for being my friend.

LINDA: Just remember that as crazy as all this is, I've gotten to see who you are and I love you. Not for being anything. Just for being you. Trusting that this letter reaches you in the best of health. God bless! P.S. I look forward to your letters!!!

WIL: Because of you I want to be a better person. I want help others so they can become better. I want to be a good example.

Twenty Dollars a Week

On Valentine's Day, February 1975 Wil told Linda he was in love with her. She told him she felt the same way and started sending him twenty dollars a week, which Wil used to better himself. However, unbeknownst to Linda, he used the money she sent him to gamble. He used his winnings to buy snacks and enroll in prison classes for his GED. Wil was smart enough to take full advantage of his new situation with Linda. His next step was to take the college entrance exams so he could register for college courses. He was determined to do the work and get a degree. He applied himself to his studies and made the Dean's list, which impressed his girlfriend, Linda.

Wil started reaching out to other Native American prisoners, some of whom he had to physically protect from inmates' racial and sexual abuse. He advocated for Native American religious rights, asking prison officials to let them grow their hair long and have sweat lodge ceremonies. Finally acting on his God-given gifts, Wil became an advocate-warrior for his people. For those who needed him to physically protect them, he was a hero. For those who needed motivation to retain their culture, he was an inspirational figure.

That summer, when Linda and her family went on their annual vacation to visit the Southwest, she got permission to visit Wil at the penitentiary. Linda was about to meet her prisoner pen pal face to face. Only one thing worried her; she was nervous about whether or not Wil would find her attractive.

Chapter Twenty

MODEL PRISONER, BAD PAROLEE

 *Wil*

For this is the will of God, that by doing good you may put to silence the ignorance of foolish men—as free, yet not using liberty as a cloak for vice, but as bondservants of God.

1 Peter 2:15-16

> *"My name is Wil and I am unable to control myself."*

Not many people can say they met their spouse when they were behind bars in prison. But this is how Linda and I met. We saw each other for the first time in the prison's Hospitality Center. We spoke to one another as if we were the only people in the room. Both of us were very happy. After that, I was a model prisoner. I took college classes and received an Associates of Arts degree in

Social Science. Linda helped me get on the right track. If it were not for Linda, I would not have a college education.

In 1976, I became eligible for parole. I came up with a good plan to present to the parole board. I was going to work in Albuquerque with the National Indian Youth Council for the summer. I made sure the parole board knew that the mission of the NIYC was "to provide and ensure that every Native American person has an equal opportunity to participate, excel and become a viable member and asset to his/her community." My goal was to get involved with the kind of government leadership and economic development that helped Native Americans gain dignity and self-respect.

Selling a Firearm in Bar While on Paraole

In the fall, I planned to go to Ohio and continue my education at the University of Cincinnati. Linda and I were making plans to be married. The parole board was impressed with my plan, and in June 1976, I was once again on the outside. I thought I had it made. I thought I would never see the inside of a prison again.

I was paroled to a halfway house in Albuquerque where I met up with a few friends from Santa Fe. I wanted to please my friends, so I began to act like the old Roho. The changes people saw in me were only on the surface. I had not changed on the inside. I forgot about Linda, forgot about my job at NIYC, and forgot to call upon Jesus when I was tempted.

I had only worked two days when we started drinking. Then one of my parolee buddies gave me a gun. As a parolee I was not allowed to possess a firearm, but I didn't care. I went to a bar with a girl and tried to sell the gun so we could pay our bar tab. The bartender called the police and I was arrested. They found out I was a parolee, so on top of being arrested for parole violation, I was also arrested for a new criminal charge—carrying a firearm in a bar.

I stayed at the Berndillo County Jail for about a month and

then was sent back to Santa Fe. I was sentenced to another one to five years and given a new number, #25939. I couldn't believe that I had messed up my life once again. I felt that I was no good. I thought I had lost Linda for good. What woman would continue to believe in me after I had betrayed her in such a callous manner?

Even though I had hurt Linda so badly, she continued to have compassion toward me. We had been making plans for two years and then I ruined everything. She learned she could not trust me, yet she still believed that if I truly surrendered to Jesus Christ, I could be a man of God. She would not give up.

After this, I didn't want to write to Linda anymore. I couldn't stand the thought of hurting her again. I was without hope and believed I would never change. At this time, I believed I was doomed to fail over and over again. I knew I was not right for Linda.

Without Jesus, there was no escaping my addictions. I had tried to do it on my own with education and good intentions, but apart from Jesus Christ, I was NOTHING. Though I was educated, I had not yet learned that very important lesson.

Linda, age three

. . . Linda Amyx and her companions

Smiling 6-Year-Old Shut-In Has Many Allies In Fight For Health

by LEE WILKES

One would think that little Linda Lee Amyx could never smile again. She has spent over a third of her six years flat on her back in a bed, a victim of rheumatic fever. But even though Linda is confined to her bed without a crowd of youngsters her own age around, she is far from lonesome. She has 68 beautiful dolls by her side and she has what she terms "The prettiest doctor in the whole world."

Strong Friend

The doctor is Dr. W. P. Borca, whose office isn't far away at 215 West Wyoming avenue in Lockland. Linda lives with her par-

at 227 North Cooper avenue. Dr. Borca isn't only a physician, however, as far as Linda is concerned, He's a travelling friend. The walls of her room are covered with pictures that the doctor has drawn for her.

Oct. 7, 1954

The article about Linda's illness

The Amyx home in Ohio

Mr. and Mrs. Amyx

Chilooco School for Indians

Wil Yazzie, student

Wil, University of Cincinnati student

The photo Linda sent to Wil
when he was behind bars
in the Santa Fe Peniteniary

Wil and Linda Yazzie, newlyweds

Wil's mother and his stepdad

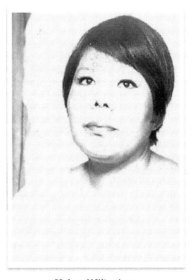

Helen, Wil's sister

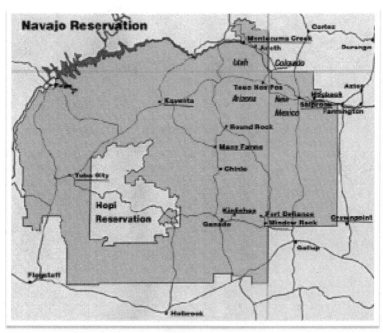

Navajo reservation map

Wil Yazzie

Wilford Yazzie
Actor, Social Worker, Minister

Wil and Gary Busey   Wil and Lindsay Wagner

Wil and Linda Thanksgiving 2010

CHRIST IS THE ANSWER MINISTRIES

CITA logo, artwork, Linda Yazzie

Chapter Twenty-One

FAMILIAR SINS

 *Jodie*

Now the works of the flesh are evident, which are: adultery, fornication, uncleanness, lewdness, idolatry, sorcery, hatred, contentions, jealousies, outbursts of wrath, selfish ambitions, dissensions, heresies, envy, murders, drunkenness, revelries, and the like; of which I tell you beforehand, just as I also told you in time past, that those who practice such things will not inherit the kingdom of God.

Galatians 5: 19–21

In 1976, Wil, the convict, was granted parole. The right people had taken note of his efforts to better himself. They liked what they heard and liked what they saw. Good behavior, such as Wil's, can go a long way in an overcrowded prison. Only his official prison records can say for sure why he was granted access to an internship program at the National Indian Youth Center. Clearly, it was an excellent opportunity for an ex-con working on his college degree in social work. It seemed reasonable and well timed.

However, Wil's constructive reprieve lasted exactly two days. Unfortunately, Wil's thirst for alcohol separated him from any kind of right thinking. A string of bad decisions started with a familiar voice calling out, "Hey, Roho! Come with us!"

For Wil, there was no escaping his past. The invitation to backslide came from a fellow ex-con. His friend didn't have to apply much pressure to convince Wil good times were about to be had. Any link to his drinking days Wil welcomed with open arms.

This part of Wil's story is hard to acknowledge because it appears as though he eagerly abandoned the goodness in his life for a short-lived party. And the truth is, he did just that. The battle was brief. Addiction won. Scripture warns us, *"Your enemy the devil prowls around like a roaring lion looking for someone to devour."* (1 Peter 5:8) In this case, the enemy didn't have to look very hard.

The night Wil reconnected with a bunch of alcoholics and ex-cons in a flophouse in Albuquerque he drank until he passed out. He woke up facing a Native American girl from Wisconsin who was also a fugitive on the run from the FBI. She convinced him it would be a good idea to go to a bar even though they had no money.

"Here's a gun. You can sell it. Pay me when you can," someone suggested.

With something to sell and the enemy coaxing him, Wil and his new drinking buddy went into a bar where he felt comfortably drunk enough to demonstrate the power of his newly acquired merchandise. He fired off a few shots and missed the chance to accidently kill someone. But he did get arrested after the bartender called the cops.

Parolee Yazzie was arrested for possession of an illegal firearm and attempting to sell it in an establishment where liquor is sold. On top of these new charges, Wil was also charged with violating the conditions of his parole. Not surprisingly, his prison sentences were about to be multiplied.

After the officials were done with him, he was scheduled to serve fourteen years to satisfy three sets of stacked up charges -- stealing a car, escaping from prison, and selling an illegal firearm while violating parole. If he had been in the correctional system when the "three strikes and you're in for life" policy was in place, Wil would not have a story to tell outside of prison life.

This, of course, was devastating news for Linda. Wil was supposed to go to University not back to prison. Everything had spiraled out of control so quickly. With the Lord's help and constant prayer, Linda was able to work through a completely new set of challenges. Remarkably, she wanted to continue her long-distance relationship with her prison pen pal and soul mate, Wil. For her, there was no choice. She had fallen in love with an alcoholic, and love, as we all know, covers a multitude of sins.

Chapter Twenty-Two

CAN'T GIVE UP

 *Linda*

I am weary with my groaning; all night I make my bed swim; I drench my couch with my tears..

Psalm 6:6

*"My name is Linda
and I am hurting."*

I was so happy when Wil made parole. I was making plans for the fall when he would come to Cincinnati. Even though he wanted to be a social worker, I still believed God planned for him to be a minister. As soon as he got out of prison, he called me from his sister's home in Albuquerque. I had embroidered a shirt for him and sent it to her to give to Wil as a celebratory present. His sister took his picture wearing it and I could hardly wait to see it.

But after a few days, I began to worry. Wil had stopped calling and there were no letters. But I imagined he was busy working, so I intensified my prayers that the Lord would keep him safe. Although the Lord heard and answered my prayers about keeping him safe, He cannot violate our free will. Wil was free to choose between good and evil. I didn't realize it at the time, but Wil only believed in Jesus Christ with his head, not his heart. This was a problem that would continue to jeopardize our relationship for several years.

A week later, I received a phone call from Wil. He had been arrested for having a gun in a bar. Of course, this violated the conditions of his parole. All our plans had suddenly evaporated in one phone call. I was devastated and couldn't stop crying. I remember taking long walks and praying, "Lord, what do I do now? What do I do now!?"

My family was relieved that it happened before he came to Cincinnati and caused embarrassment for us. They believed this parole violation would be the end of our love and that my eyes would be opened. My family was convinced he was using me. They only wanted the best for me and wanted to protect me, which I understood but did not appreciate. A part of me wanted to give up, but another part of me still loved him and still believed God had a plan for his life. God's plan, I believed, included Wil and me—and ministry. I couldn't shake the belief that the Lord had called Wil to be a minister.

After many, many tears and prayers, I decided I could not give up on Wil. I knew Wil was used to people giving up on him. He was used to people abandoning him. It had happened throughout his whole life. I also knew he had given up on himself. I wanted to show him that Jesus had not given up on him. I wanted to prove to him that love doesn't give up and that love bears all things.

I decided what the enemy meant for bad, the Lord would use for good. Even then I believed these circumstances would one day become stories we would share with others. I had faith to believe that one day Wil would have a powerful testimony, one that would demonstrate the delivering power of Jesus. I had God's peace knowing our love had a genuine foundation. So, I wrote to Wil and told him I still loved him. I told him we had come too far to give up hope. I wanted to go on building our relationship.

I knew we had a future together. In my heart, I just knew.

REPEAT OFFENDER

 *Wil*

No one can serve two masters; for either he will hate the one and love the other, or else he will be loyal to the one and despise the other. You cannot serve God and mammon

Matthew 6:24

*"My name is Wil Yazzie
and I am incarcerated—again!"*

I became a resident of the New Mexico prison system for a second time. In a sense, I was institutionalized. I felt at home with people I knew there. All I had ever known was boarding school, reformatory, jails and prison. I started to wonder if I was one of those habitual criminals—a "lifer" who only finds security in prison.

Everyone I had known in the free world had forsaken me. I had no letters or visitors except for Linda. I couldn't understand why she continued to love me. I was ready to give up but she wasn't. Once more, we began to write our daily letters.

One would think that this time I would finally surrender my life to the Lord. But it was the same old thing in prison. I went to chapel and Bible study and continued to gamble. Like many people, I thought church attendance meant salvation. I thought I could still hold onto my worldly interests. I believed in Jesus, but He was not the Lord of my life.

I liked working with my hands, so I stopped my college classes to work in the furniture making section of the prison industry. I earned $.24 cents an hour. Combined with Linda's financial help, I was able to continue gambling. It was easy to quit smoking marijuana. Gambling was an addiction that began in my childhood. It was a stuborn enemy and a very difficult habit to break.

Becoming a Reformer

When I first arrived to prison in 1974, I decided to become involved with my fellow Native American inmates. I wanted to improve our circumstances. When I was on "the outside," I belonged to the Southwestern chapter of AIM (American Indian Movement), so I was already a registered activist. We sued the state of New Mexico, the Secretary of Corrections and the warden for not allowing our traditional religious beliefs to be practiced in prison. For example, we were forced to cut our hair. We won our lawsuit, which opened doors for non-Natives to choose their hairstyle.

I became the president of the Native American prison group. We called the group "Refined Navajo." It was formed with the intent to heal the inner person. We held the first prison pow-wow at Santa Fe and also had a Navajo wedding for one of the inmates and his girlfriend. The group gave us unity in prison, which we shared with Mexican inmates. For whatever reason, when there were altercations among the different races, the Natives and Mexicans stuck up for one another.

We asked for medicine men to be allowed in so they could

conduct our sweat lodge ceremonies.[4] Native prisoners wanted to repair damage done to their spirits, minds and bodies in this fashion. I became immersed in our traditional beliefs. But because of Linda, I wanted to hang onto Jesus. I wanted to please both my Native brothers and Linda. Because of my divided heart, I was not being true to anyone, including myself. For many years, I did not understand that as a Christian I could not worship other gods.

If only I had stuck to the one true God, I would have been spared decades of agony. If I had only understood the difference between believing in Jesus and belonging to Jesus, Linda and her family would not have had to endure so much pain and suffering.

---

4   The sweat lodge is a place of spiritual refuge and mental and physical healing, a place to get answers and guidance by asking spiritual entities, totem helpers, the Creator and Mother Earth for needed wisdom and power.

Chapter Twenty-Four

WEAPON OF CHOICE

 *Jodie*

For the weapons of our warfare are not carnal but mighty in God for pulling down strongholds.

2 Corinthians 10:4

With good reason to question the final outcome but unwilling to terminate her devotion to Wil, Linda returned to her letter writing campaign. She never ran out of things to write about. Her letters included mundane details highlighting her family's daily routines, the going-ons of her sister Frankie and brother-in-law Harold and her younger sister Nancy. A passionate animal lover, Linda would also chronicle the antics of all their dogs. She wrote about the usual and unusual stuff that went on at work, how Brother Patterson's Sunday sermons affected her and everything else that went on at her beloved Wesleyan Christian Church, a church her grandparents helped start in 1936.

Having come from an extremely sheltered life, Linda was often told she was a bit backward. Because she was employee at the school where her school records were kept, she couldn't resist the temptation to find out what her teachers had said about her. She uncovered phrases such as "Linda is a good student but she puts up walls," confirming that her shy nature contributed to her predilection for letter writing. For Linda, communicating on paper made it much easier for her to share personal concerns.

"Wil and I might never have gotten along if we had met in person," Linda admitted. "I would have been too shy."

Linda's Favorite Book

Since childhood, Linda's favorite book has always been *The Bird's Christmas Carol,* written by Kate Douglas Wiggins in 1887. In fact, she never fails to read it every year. Wiggin, who also wrote *Rebecca of Sunnybrook Farm,* tells the heartwarming story of the Bird family's special Christmas baby whom they named Carol. Though Carol is a sickly little girl, she is unusually loving and generous. The young girl had a positive effect on everyone with whom she came into contact.

At the age of five, Carol contracts an unspecified illness, and by the time she is ten, she is bedridden. Physicians had to tell her parents that she does not have long to live. Sound familiar?

Charitable giving, as a way to happiness, is one of the more recognizable themes in the novel. However, Linda took hold of another ideal. She was impressed by how each week the little girl sent books and wrote letters to other ill children stuck in hospital beds. Each Saturday, Carol chose ten books, which became her circulating library. She slipped in cards that said: *"Please keep this book two weeks and read it. With love, Carol Bird."* Then Mrs. Bird took the books to the Children's Hospital and brought home the ones she had left there two weeks earlier.

The author writes:

This was a source of great happiness; for some of the Hospital children that were old enough to print or write, and strong enough to do it, wrote Carol cunning little letters about the books, and she answered them, and they grew to be friends. (It is very funny, but you do not always

*have to see people to love them. Just think about it, and see
if it isn't so.)*

Again, does this sound familiar?

Linda continued to send Wil words of encouragement along
with spending money. She had always encouraged Wil to read the
Bible and attend church while he was incarcerated, but after his
plight had expanded, Linda quickly realized Wil's relationship
with Jesus stemmed from his mind, not his spirit.

Compelled to Pray

According to Linda, Wil needed to get genuinely saved.
Sending letters with practical gifts and scripture verses wasn't
enough. Linda knew she had to pray.

*Dear Lord, please send your precious Holy Spirit. Get a
hold of Wil's heart so he can accept you as his savior and
receive forgiveness for his sins. Deliver him from evil and
separate him from alcohol. In Jesus' name, Amen.*

Linda, a devoted student of God's Word, understood God
always has the big picture in mind. Although it is hard for people
to let go of the present and have faith for the future, years of Bible
study had taught Linda that God uses adversity to bring people
to faith. Linda was well aware of how God doesn't waste trials or
painful shipwrecks. She knew that when the Apostle Paul survived
terrifying shipwrecks and poisonous snakebites, unbelievers came
to recognize the power of God. The challenge for Christians is to
have faith for a better future and rise from the wreckage like Paul.
Disciples of Christ illuminate the way to the Savior, which is the
reason Linda was not willing to sit on the sidelines full of self-pity
just because Wil had fallen off the wagon.

Instead, she went to her heavenly Father in prayer and
praised God for His mysterious ways. She thanked Him for her
unexpected trial. She praised Him for what must have felt like
a shipwreck of a situation. She continued to ask God for Wil's
salvation, and she wasn't going to stop believing God for a total

transformation until Wil was truly born again.

"*Therefore, if anyone is in Christ, he is a new creation; old things have passed away; behold, all things have become new..*"

2 Corinthians 5:17 was one of Linda's Bible favorite verses.

"*Dear Wil, Humble yourself in the sight of the Lord, and He shall lift you up,*" she would write. Faithful Linda sprinkled her letters with scripture verses, always careful to speak the truth in love. She was compelled not only by the love she had for Wil, but also by the love of Christ, which told her he had been lied to enough in his life. He deserved to hear the truth—everyone does.

Pray Always

Linda Amyx grew up praying. The Amyx family were church people who rarely missed a Sunday morning, Sunday evening or Wednesday evening church service. Linda's family prayed at every meal and everywhere in between. Her parents were potent examples of prayer warriors. No doubt they planted many godly seeds for their daughter's future spouse long before she was old enough to be a bride.

Lord, may our daughter's future spouse love you with all his heart, soul, mind and strength, and know Jesus as his savior. May he love our daughter with a faithful, undying love for as long as they both shall live. May he recognize his body is the temple of the Holy Spirit and treat it wisely. May he have admirable goals for his life. May he use his talents for Your Glory and may they complement one another as they enjoy one another. May he establish their home in accordance with Your prescribed order as outlined in Your Holy Word. Lord, bring this partner to our daughter in Your perfect timing so that there would be no doubt that You created them for each other. In Jesus' Name, Amen.

Naturally, prayer was Linda's weapon of choice against her unseen foe, and it seemed to be working. Wil went back to his studies and found more positive things to do.

Chapter Twenty-Four

Wil and Linda Wed

After serving only two additional years to his compounded sentence, Wil was miraculously paroled. Upon his release, he traveled to Ohio where Linda lived with her family in their home in Lockland. Finally, Linda and her family would experience Wil Yazzie outside prison walls.

Wil and Linda's love for one another was officially acknowledged on September 1, 1978, when they were joined together as man and wife by Linda's longtime pastor, Reverend Eugene Campbell. The special occasion was untarnished by Wil's troubled past. If anything, their marriage served as a gravestone to Roho. Linda Amyx had, indeed, brought out the best in Wil Yazzie.

Chapter Twenty-Five

HOME SWEET HOME

 *Wil*

So husbands ought to love their own wives as their own bodies; he who loves his wife loves himself.

Ephesians 5:28

"I am Wil Yazzie and I am a newlywed and a college student living in Ohio."

In 1978, I came before the parole board. Linda had sent a letter confirming that we were going to be married and would be living in her mother's home in Ohio. I was already enrolled in the University of Cincinnati, although it was not my first choice. Believe it or not, my first choice was God's Bible School. I convinced Linda (and myself) that I was a Christian because I went to church services and Bible studies in prison. I thought I was "living for the Lord."

Matthew 7:14 says, *"But small is the gate and narrow is the road that leads to life, and only a few find it."* One must live a holy life and I wasn't. I was gambling, using foul language and heavily involved with traditional religious beliefs, all of which was an indication that I was not a real Christian. I wasn't on the road Jesus spoke of; I was hanging around the gate. Because my thinking was so distorted, I engaged in many selfish behaviors and had many foolish thoughts.

For example, I believed I was called to be an evangelist. I wanted to help others when I was the one who needed the most help. My application for admission at God's Bible School was denied even though Linda talked to one of the deans trying to convince them that I was a changed man. They refused to accept me. I was angry and couldn't understand why I was being rejected. But I know now the Holy Spirit had guided them with wisdom. I was definitely not ready for God's Bible School.

Nevertheless, Linda and I were so full of joy knowing that we were about to start our new lives together. Linda, her mom and younger sister fixed up a small apartment for us in their basement. I lived there, alone, until two weeks later when Linda and I were married on September 1st. We had a small wedding with just Linda's family and my friends, Robert and Ann Parks, the couple who helped me in Farmington. They flew in from Chicago to be with us. They were happy to share in our celebration and very pleased to see that I had turned my life around.

After a reception at our home, we had a two-day honeymoon at a hotel in downtown Cincinnati. Linda was working as a librarian's aide at a public school down the street from our home. Her new school year started the day after Labor Day. She was so happy to return with a new name—Mrs. Yazzie.

Full-Time University Student

My classes began in October at the University of Cincinnati. I decided to become a social worker after my dream of becoming an evangelist fell apart. I took twelve credits. Classes were easy for me. I told my professors that things were done differently on the reservation and they took my word for it. When it came to my coursework, I was given some leeway. I was light years ahead of my classmates in personal knowledge concerning addictions and other issues a social worker faces. I lied to my professors and I think they believed me because I was a Native American living off the reservation.

Linda and I were very happy in our small basement apartment. I couldn't wait to get home each day. While I studied, she did her artwork. Then we would watch television together. I enjoyed sport programs and Linda happily tolerated them. We were active in our church and joined the choir. We felt very loved and supported by everyone. A couple weeks after we were married, the women of the church gave us a wedding shower. I joined the church softball team and coached a local little league team. I loved working with the children. On Saturdays, we went to ball games and then treated the boys to ice cream.

During this time, we were very close to Linda's family. We joined her older sister, Frankie, and her husband, Harold, on day trips. One of my favorite trips was traveling an hour and half south to the Kentucky Horse Park in Lexington. Life was good. Very good. One would think my troubles were over and that I had settled into marital bliss, but my divided heart caught up with me.

We had been married a few short weeks when I started drinking again. It wasn't constant drinking as it had been in the southwest. After all, I was a full-time student and had to maintain a high grade point average in order to keep my scholarships. I would actually go a few weeks without taking a drink, then I would go on a bender.

What's That Smell?

The first time I came home after drinking, Linda ran to the door to give me a "Welcome home, honey!" kiss. She smelled the alcohol but had no idea what it was. She came from a Christian family where they would sooner put poison on the dinner table than a bottle of liquor. I told her that I had put some after-shave lotion on at a store downtown. She wrinkled her nose and said, "Don't ever use that again. It stinks!"

It wasn't long before she learned what the smell was. She cried and looked so sad. I hated what I was doing to her. Even though I previously had no respect for women, I respected Linda. I controlled my language around her. She never heard me say an offensive word. She never saw me smoke or take a drink. I wish I could say she never saw me drunk, but that's how I came home many nights.

The 1979 college year ended in May and I got a summer job at General Motors. My employment there lasted only one week. I got drunk one day after work and went home. Linda and her family were gone. They had persuaded Linda to go with them on a Florida vacation, which they had planned for months. They were afraid that I would hurt Linda if I came home in a drunken rage and she was alone. Although I abused her emotionally, I never once thought about hurting her physically.

The next-door neighbor told me where they were, and for some reason, gave me a bottle of liquor. In my drunken state, I decided to go to the airport and fly home to New Mexico. I stayed there most of the summer, drinking with my old Renegade friends.

Summer Booze Break

Times had changed. Most of my fellow gang members had either died or gotten married. Alcohol and drugs had taken their toll. Instead of an organized gang, we were just a sorry bunch of drunks hanging out together.

Linda had no idea where I was or what had happened. After returning home from Florida and realizing I was gone, she resigned herself to the fact that our marriage was over. I did not contact her all summer.

It was late September and my plan was to return home and start the new school year at the University of Cincinnati. The National Indian Youth Council bought a bus ticket for me, but when I arrived in Cincinnati, Linda wasn't willing to reconcile as if nothing had happened. She had grown up. She knew that her fairy tale dream would have no happy ending if things continued as they were. I took a sleeping room close to campus.

All through September Linda and I went on "dates." I talked her into giving me another chance. We thought that if we had our own place things would be better, so we rented a small apartment where I could take a bus to campus and Linda would be able to walk to the school where she worked. We moved into our new apartment on Linda's birthday, November 1, 1979. We were full of hope thinking our new place was a new beginning for us.

Happy Couple

Every day when I returned home from class, Linda would have supper waiting for me. As a couple, we were very happy. We were so excited about the holidays that year, we put up a Christmas tree before Thanksgiving. Linda was (and is) an avid animal lover and really missed having a dog. Since our lease had a "no cats or dogs" clause, we decided to find a caged animal of some kind. On Christmas Eve, we went to K-Mart and found one lone brown guinea pig left in the store. We bought her and named her Buffy because she had a big head and looked like a buffalo. We spent Christmas Eve night, Christmas Day and New Year's Eve with Linda's family. Of course, Buffy was a part of each gathering. I remember thinking, "It's going to be the best year ever! I'm so happy!"

I managed to stay sober during those months of November and December in our new home. Linda was beginning to relax and no longer worried whether or not I would be home that afternoon. We purchased a used car so I could drop her off at work each morning, go to classes and pick her up afterwards.

One Day I'll Surrender

I can honestly say with all my heart, I wanted to be a good husband. Once again, we became active in our church. We went to revival meetings. It was there I realized I was playing games with God. I would feel guilty when the altar calls were given because I did not respond. Instead, I resolved to stay sober on my own.

make it without me.

Compounding Mistakes

Then my sister died in February 1980. The news of her death shocked me. We had been every close. People thought we were twins when we were in school. She visited me once in prison and I went to her home for a short visit after my release in 1976. Unfortunately, Linda and I didn't have enough money for me to go to Albuquerque for her funeral, so like a true alcoholic, I took up drinking again and blamed the situation for my helplessness.

A few weeks later, it was spring break. I dropped off Linda at work as usual. But instead of doing what I normally did, I decided to drive downtown so I could hang around Fountain Square, a meeting place where working people ate their lunches from brown paper bags. I enjoyed meeting and talking to people, but instead of enjoying the people and the scenery, I went into a bar and bought a drink for somebody I didn't know. While he was drinking, I remembered the warmth of alcohol and the nice feeling it gave me as it went through my system. I decided to buy a shot for myself.

My first mistake was going into the bar. My second mistake was buying liquor. My third mistake was drinking the shot of whiskey and thinking I could limit my drinking.

I got drunk and decided to go to the University to see what was happening. That was the biggest mistake of the night. The campus police had to arrest me for public intoxication.

It was very hard to face Linda when she and her sister came down to pick me up at the jail. I could see that Linda had been crying and that she was under a great deal of stress. Upsetting Linda was not a good thing to do because of her damaged heart.

My punishment was to check into a local rehab center for a month. Either our pastor or a teacher friend of Linda's would take her to see me each day after she got off work. I was unrepentant and defiant. I blamed Linda because I couldn't go to my sister's funeral. I said some cruel things to her during the family sessions. Even as I said these horrible things, I felt sorry for Linda. But

I could not bring myself to tell her I didn't mean it. Deep down I knew everything was my fault.

I Abandon My Sweet Wife

I was released from rehab on April 7. Two days later, I dropped Linda off at work. She stopped at the steps, turned around and waved good-bye. I don't know what she was thinking, but that image of Linda smiling and waving is something I will never forget. Maybe I was so impressed because I wouldn't see Linda again for twenty-eight years.

I immediately went downtown and got drunk. I wrecked our car and abandoned it. I had been hanging around downtown for a couple of days when something remarkable happened. Early one morning, I was walking down an alley. I was passing time, waiting for the bars to reopen. (Back then bars were open 23 hours a day. They closed from 5:00 a.m. until 6:00 a.m. for cleaning.) I heard a moan and saw something moving out of the corner of my eye. I thought an animal might be trapped in the nearby snow pile, but it was an elderly woman. She had passed out and fallen down, or perhaps she had fallen and then passed out. In any case, I tried to wake her up.

It took some time but she finally responded. I asked her where she lived and then took her to her tiny apartment. I made some coffee and made sure she was all right before I left. I am certain she was like me, a drunk who would have frozen to death if someone had not found her. If I had not intervened, she would have died a "Cincinnati popsicle." Looking back, I thank God that He used me to save her life.

Stealing from Linda

I returned to the University's financial aid office where I picked up my scholarship checks. I had taken Linda's credit card and charged items on it so I would have stuff to sell on the streets. I bought a plane ticket and headed back to the southwest.

This time there was no going home.

I left Ohio and abandoned my sweet wife Linda—and for what? I left everything to pursue my own personal living hell, or as other people called it, the 1980's.

Chapter Twenty-Six

PRINCE NOT SO CHARMING

He heals the brokenhearted and binds up their wounds.

Psalm 147:3

*"My name is Linda Amyx Yazzie
and I am a divorcee."*

When I got married, a part of me still believed in fairy tales. Wil was my Prince Charming. The day I married Wil I was over the moon in love. I loved Wil with all my heart and I was so happy to finally be Mrs. Wilford Yazzie.

My mom did everything she could to convince me not to marry Wil, but I could see no fault in him. Even on the morning of our wedding she told me it wasn't too late to back out. I wailed, "Mom, it's my wedding day!"

I am sure there were very few dry eyes at our wedding. I must have looked terribly vulnerable standing at the altar, putting my life into the hands of my imperfect husband. But I trusted Wil completely. We had the thirteenth chapter of First Corinthians read at our wedding and I believed every word about the power of love.

Unshakable Faith

Despite the fact that Wil began drinking so soon after our wedding, I still was happy and filled with an unshakeable faith in the Lord that everything between us was going to work out. I believed Wil's "incidents" would lead him to make a full surrender to the Lord, and in time, he would become a minister. I remember the shame of returning to school after an incident and telling my co-workers not to worry, my prayers would be answered soon enough. I told them I was encouraged because Wil had repented. I told myself it would never happen again. But, of course, it did.

Nevertheless, we had so many good times. I knew Wil loved me and that alcohol controlled him. It was plain to see he was caught in the relentless grip of a terrible addiction. I could tell there were many times in church when he was under great conviction. His body would tremble slightly as he held onto the pew in front of him. He just could not give his heart to Jesus. He believed he could go to church and still manage his double life. Seeing that the Holy Spirit is a gentleman, meaning He never forces His way into someone's life, it was up to Wil to take action.

Blinders Start to Come Off

Many of Wil's childhood wounds were not revealed to me during our courtship. For example, I had no idea that he was sexually abused as a child. I think he was afraid to tell me because I had no concept of the depths of sin he had experienced in his life. I knew nothing about his gang life in Farmington. Once in anger, he told me about gambling in prison and what my money really went for, but I had blinders on. I believed that one day he would abandon all his bad habits. I was one hundred percent in love with him and nothing could shake my faith.

The blinders started to come when he left in the summer of 1979. It took awhile for that hurt to heal. During our short separation, we decided to live on our own and not under the same roof with my family. I wanted to give Wil another opportunity to show his love to me. I also wanted to give him another chance to get genuinely saved. We were a young couple in love, so getting back together and finding our own apartment was the only thing we could do.

We moved into our own place and truly couldn't have been any happier. We had so much fun finding used furniture and decorating things, making the home just the way we liked. We enjoyed going to church, singing in the choir, attending University of Cincinnati basketball games and taking the pastor's daughter out to eat afterwards. We enjoyed each other's company and spent all our free time together.

Our landlord did not allow dogs or cats, which I did not like at all. But nothing was mentioned about having (or not having) a caged animal, so we went out on Christmas Eve and bought a guinea pig. We named her Buffy. She was the cutest thing. She used to wake us up in the mornings by whistling. Imagine—a whistling guinea pig for an alarm clock!

Planning Our Future

Wil and I were doing great. We were so in love. Because of my health problems, we knew we weren't going to have children of our own, so we discussed the possibility of adopting Native American children. We had settled down and it made sense to start making plans for our future together. And everything was fine until he got drunk and was arrested for public intoxication.

Wil was ordered to go to rehab and get counseling. As his spouse, I had to attend family counseling sessions. It was a twelve-step program with an emphasis on reaching out to a Higher Power. Any Higher Power was acceptable. If your Higher Power happened to be Mickey Mouse or Mother Nature, that was good enough for this program, which is why I knew the program wouldn't help Wil. He was still a dog chained to a tree. The chain had to be broken, and the only one who could break the chain in a permanent fashion was Jesus.

He said some things at the counseling sessions that hurt me deeply. I knew he was slipping away, so I thought if I told him how much I loved and needed him, he would stick with me. Maybe that's what drove him away. I was beginning to cling to him too much and it was starting to get on his nerves. He couldn't tolerate my tears anymore.

He Didn't Even Say Good-Bye

I got off work one day in April 1980 and there was no Wil waiting in the car to take me home. So I walked home and fixed his favorite supper—fried chicken, mashed potatoes and green beans. Later, when I walked into our mid-week prayer meeting alone, everyone knew something was wrong. After the meeting, some dear friends offered to go look for him even though it was pouring down rain.

We searched for Wil in the Rhine, one of Cincinnati's skid row slum areas. By midnight, we knew our efforts were in vain. My friends brought me back to our apartment to get a change of clothing and Buffy. They were concerned for my safety. They dropped me off at my mom's house. They thought that if Wil returned home during night, he might hurt me even though I told them Wil had never laid a hand on me.

My family insisted I get a divorce. I agreed to go to a lawyer for a legal separation but I didn't want to divorce Wil. I still loved him and harbored a secret desire that one day he would come back a changed person. Wil was (and still is) the only man I have ever loved. The pressure from my family was overwhelming, so I finally agreed to a divorce. My loved ones convinced me that being married to Wil was a mistake as well as a financial liability. I went back to my maiden name, Linda Amyx, and returned to our family home to live with my mother and younger sister.

People kept telling me I should forget that part of my life, but of course, I couldn't.

I think the lowest point was when I had to tell my co-workers at school. I was devastated when a teacher told me, "I bet you don't believe in God now!" I felt like a complete failure. I began to think that I had failed the Lord and began to question whether I misunderstand the Lord's will about marrying Wil?

My anxiety was like a dark cloud hanging over my life until one day the Lord gave me His peace, the kind that passes all human understanding. After that, when people would say, "You made a big mistake when you married Wil," I would reply, "No, Wil made a big mistake when he left me." I held on to the belief that God still had a plan for both our lives, even though the wounds Wil had created were still very fresh.

In 1981, I received a letter saying he was back in prison in Santa Fe. I wrote him a letter to tell me I was divorcing him. For a few years, I received a Christmas card from him but there was never a return address. Somehow it helped to know that he still remembered our Christmas celebrations and all the fun we had. It also helped to know my sister Frankie believed in our marriage. One time after he left, I remember saying to Frankie, "Everything was a lie. It was all lies! He didn't love me."

"No, that's not right!" Frankie told me. "Wil loves you."

Then Frankie told me about the time when I was sick and she and Wil took me to the doctor's office. While Frankie and Wil waited for me, Wil told Frankie, "If anything happens to Linda, I would be devastated. I can't live without her."

It was so nice to hear such positive encouragement. I could not shake the feeling that God had a purpose for us as a couple. I was also under the belief that the enemy wanted to destroy Wil, along with our marriage.

Over the years, after Wil left the marriage so he could drink, the Holy Spirit would impress upon me from time to time that Wil was in danger. I would immediately start praying for him. This often happened in the middle of the night. I would wake up feeling compelled to pray. I never told anyone about these times.

I thought they would think I was crazy. Truth be told, I was praying for my husband who had cold-heartedly deserted me.

No One But Wil

Some may find this hard to believe, but I forgave Wil the day he left. My Christian faith enabled me to pardon Wil's terrible behavior, and my deep love for him enabled me to pray on a daily basis.

There were men who asked me out on dates but I always refused. I could never love anybody but Wil. Why would I want to waste my time and their money on a date that would mean nothing to me? Dating was not for me. I felt I was still married in the eyes of God. On some occasions, I even wore my wedding ring, the turquoise band Wil had given to me when he was mostly known by his number: Prisoner #22486. But the years were passing by and there was no word from Wil.

I had no idea if he was even alive, but I felt that he must be because the Lord continued to prompt me to pray for him. I assumed he had most likely remarried, so I stopped praying that he would return to me. Instead, I prayed that before he died he would repent. Even if our reunion took place in heaven, I believed Wil and I would see each other again.

> *"Dear Lord, I know I'm not a part of Wil's life, but please Lord, before he dies, bring Him to you. Don't let him go to hell."*

I remember being at a family reunion and talking with a woman who asked me, "Are you married?"

"Yes and no," I told her. "I'm divorced but I still feel married."

Then I told her all about Wil, the love of my life.

Then she asked, "Do you think you'll ever remarry?"

Not knowing my future, I told her I would never remarry.

WASTED YEARS

 *Wil*

His own iniquities entrap the wicked man, and he is caught in the cords of his sin.

Proverbs 5:22

*"My name is Wil Yazzie
and I am Satan's ally."*

After leaving Linda, I went back to New Mexico. I couldn't get away from drinking and I couldn't forget my old gang members in Farmington. I thought they needed me and I liked being their leader. It never occurred to me that Linda needed me. Satan filled my mind with other thoughts. I was a married man who had taken vows declaring that I would protect and care for Linda until death do us part. None of that mattered any more. The only thing that matter was drinking.

I went to Farmington where everyone was glad to see Roho. I was welcomed back into the fold with open arms and plenty of booze, which is the reason I stayed there for the next eight years. Unless I was behind bars, I stayed drunk every day. I remember selling my car for $150.00 to get liquor. Booze was more important than having transportation.

I'm a Homeless Bum

The Renegades gang had fallen apart, leaving me gang leader of nothing. In Farmington, I was just a homeless derelict. A number of my drinking friends had died since I had visited there in the summer of 1979. Of the original 300 gang members, there were only about 40 or 50 left.

I was arrested for larceny and then released on my own recognizance. I failed to appear in court on my appointed date. Once again, a warrant for my arrest was issued. As a repeat offender, I had put myself into dangerous territory. I didn't know that the "three strikes and you're in for life" law was in effect.

Some time later, I was apprehended and ended up before a judge for sentencing. I could have been given a life sentence but was given a light sentence for habitual offenders instead. I was sentence to one year at the state penitentiary, plus one-year probation. Even though a lighter sentence benefited me, it seemed strange.

I wrote to Linda from jail. She wrote me back and said she had filed for divorce. I could tell from her letter that she was deeply wounded and hurting very badly. I gave up communicating with her except at Christmas. I sent Christmas cards for a few years because I remembered how much she loved Christmas. I did not want to have contact with her, so I did not include a return address. I didn't want to hurt her all over again.

Missed the Most Violent Prison Riot in History

Amazingly, being given such a light sentence meant I was on the outside when one the most violent prison riots in the history of the American correctional system took place. If I had been in Sante Fe in 1980, I have no doubt I would have been one of the ones killed—or I would have killed someone. Thirty-three inmates died and more than two hundred inmates were treated for injuries. None of the twelve officers taken hostage were killed, but seven of them were treated for injuries caused by beatings and rapes. Things had significantly improved by the time I arrived in 1981. I look back now and see the Lord's hand and how He had protected me once more.

Even though I was a drunk, I still liked helping people. Some friends and I were drinking by the San Juan River at a location we referred to as "the hanging tree." One of my buddies got too far out and started yelling for help. I thought he was just playing around, but then I realized he was really drowning. I jumped in and pulled him out. I saved his life. He was very grateful I was there and that I was brave enough to jump in and rescue him.

I was thankful my dad taught me how to swim when I was a young child because I saved another man's life during this time. Again, we had been drinking; this time at The Turquoise Bar in Hogback, New Mexico. One of our friends got caught in a whirlpool current in a concrete stormwater channel. He didn't know how to swim and couldn't get out, so I dove in and got him out of the swirling water.

It wasn't long before I violated the conditions of my parole. After two months in Santa Fe, I was sent to Roswell Correctional Center in New Mexico. After four months, I had completed my sentence and was no longer was on probation. As soon as I was released, I celebrated by drinking all the way from Roswell to Farmington. I felt a sense of freedom because I was no longer on probation. Though I was no longer in the prison system, I was not released from Satan's imprisonment.

Anything to Stay Drunk

When I arrived in Farmington, I noticed there were a lot of new people. Although I didn't know who they were, they had heard of Roho. And they wanted to fight me. I no longer wanted to fight because I no longer had a gang to back me up. I tried to stay out of the way and just drink. My territory had changed. I could no longer get drinks from my so-called buddies. I had to steal in order to buy liquor.

In order to stay drunk, I had to go to Cortez, Colorado where my mother and her new husband lived. I went there because my mother would give me money. She knew I was in bad shape and that if I didn't have alcohol in me, I would go into the deadly D.T.'s. I know now that my hallucinations were demonic. Every terrifying image seemed very real. I saw dead people, insects and snakes, and everything I saw was trying kill me.

I knew Farmington and Cortez to be somewhat racist towns, and I was spending a lot of time in jail in both places. One time, at the Farmington jail, I had an alcoholic seizure and had to be resuscitated. I almost died and had to be taken to the hospital. It is hard for anyone to believe that I could be so close to death so many times and yet return to the same alcoholic life. I could have easily died alone in jail many times and no one would have even known. I would have been taken to the morgue and writen off as just another drunken Indian.

A Cry for Help

I remember begging my mother for more drinking money and she refused to give it to me. In anger, I grabbed some scissors and stabbed myself in the stomach. I didn't want to kill myself. Even in my drunken state, I knew I would go to hell and I was afraid of that. I suppose I wanted attention and to make my mom feel sorry for refusing my request for drinking money. I was taken to the hospital where they removed my appendix and stitched my wound.

Because of that incident, I can empathize with young people who cut themselves. They say they want to feel pain. Pain, they say, is a way of having control in their lives. I understand this because of what I did to myself at my mother's house. My scissors episode was a definite cry for help. I also understand why many of my friends committed suicide. Dying was easier than going through alcohol withdrawal. They didn't really want to die. They just wanted the suffering to end.

Satan's Lies, or God's Plan?

I think Satan was laughing the whole time we were drinking ourselves to death. When we were drunk, we were absent from our minds and that's when Satan took over. Satan is a liar and murderer. He is the destroyer of people's lives. One second after my friends committed suicide, they were in hell and beyond help for all eternity.

If only people would realize that one of Satan's most powerful tools is to convince people there is no hope of life being any different. Satan wants people to give up and die. Some of the people who killed themselves or died an alcohol-related death were, at one time, the nicest, most caring, and loving individuals I've ever known—that was before Satan and his demons destroyed their minds and their lives.

God has a plan for everyone's life. He sees us, all of us—even as we are being formed in our mother's wombs. He loves us and wants us to have an abundant life. I have asked myself many times, why did I let the enemy enslave me for so long? Why didn't I surrender my life to Christ when I was with Linda? Why was I spared death so many times?

I was powerless to control myself, but because of Linda's prayers, the Lord protected me. I know this now.

Chapter Twenty-Eight

WITHOUT WIL

 *Linda*

Truly my soul silently waits for God; from Him comes my salvation. He only is my rock and my salvation; He is my defense; I shall not be greatly moved..

Psalm 62: 1-2

"My name is Linda
and I am a firm believer."

Eventually, I settled into my new life as a divorcee. I have always been a happy person with a Pollyanna type personality, which is why I played "The Glad Game" even though my life had fallen apart. I refused to be depressed and upset.

For many years, it was just Mom and me. Then my older married sister, Frankie, became ill. Her complaint was that her legs hurt and she had a headache. The next morning her husband called to tell mom that Frankie couldn't stand up or see. We called 911. Frankie ended up staying in the hospital for three months. The doctors said she had some type of viral infection that had traveled into her brain. The infection, they told us, was eating up and destorying her nervous system.

It was during my sister's hospital stay that I felt called to become a minister. I started taking correspondence courses from the International Ministerial Fellowship (IMF), an association of laymen, clergypersons, and churches that "work across denominational lines to love, serve, encourage, and help enable those who are called to serve in front-line Christian ministry." IMF provided me with a spiritual covering, appropriate credentials and the opportunity for affiliation with others who share a like faith and calling.

By the end of her hospital stay, Frankie had become completely incapacitated. They never did find out what was wrong with her. Doctors told us she wouldn't live long and that she should go to a nursing home. Mom refused to allow her daughter to be sent to a nursing home. She decided she would take care of Frankie. The doctors told us that Frankie's needs were far greater than what one person could provide, meaning Mom could never do it alone.

Mom didn't hestiate. She told the doctor, "I'm not alone."

When asked who would help her, Mom answered, "The Lord will help me."

And that was the end of it. We brought Frankie home.

Divine Visitors

Frankie couldn't talk or feed herself, and although she couldn't communicate in her handicapped state, Mom, Nancy and I understood her. We had daily devotions and read the Bible every day in her room. Hours spent with Frankie were beautiful times. People came to our house to encourage Frankie, but they left encouraged by Frankie's smile. It was all she had left and it was enough. It was a blessing to be able to care for her right up until she received her ultimate healing. Frankie went to be with the Lord on August 13th, 1994, exactly nine years to the day from the day she got sick.

After Frankie's death, I continued to work at the elementary school down the street from our home. I also went to nursing homes as a volunteer minister and held church services for area residents. I really enjoyed visiting, preaching and reading the Bible with them. I was rebuilding my life without Wil and I was happy.

However, I was not finished caring for ailing family members. I became the sole caretaker for Mom through her fatal battle with her chronic lung disease and leukemia. It was such a privilege to care for Mom. She had taken care of her parents and Frankie and now it was my turn to show her how much I loved her.

The Lord knew how was hard it was for me knowing that Mom was dying, so I was blessed with a dream two weeks before she died. The dream started with a beautiful woman coming into our house. I had the sense that I knew her but I didn't. The woman said to me, "I used to worry about you and your mom, living here all alone, until I saw you had two men living with you."

I told the woman, "There are no men living with us. It's just me and mom."

"No," the woman said to me. "There are two men living with you. When I look through the window, I'm looking for you, but I also see two men walking around in the house. When your mom needed an ambulance and the EMS came for her, I saw a man by the stretcher and another man behind you."

I knew the Lord had sent His angels to be with us just when we needed them the most. And when Mom began her final journey home, I knew we were once again in the presence of God's holy angels. It wasn't just a pleasant feeling. What I felt was divinely comforting and very real. Throughout these years, while my family members were sick and dying, I experienced God's great mercy and faithfulness. He said He would never leave us or forsake us, and this was precisely the reason I couldn't stop praying for Wil.

Chapter Twenty-Nine

GET RID OF HIM

And as it is appointed for men to die once, but after this the judgment, so Christ was offered once to bear the sins of many. To those who eagerly wait for Him He will appear a second time, apart from sin, for salvation.

Hebrews 9: 27–28

*"My name is Wil
and I am miserable."*

In 1986, a friend and I hitchhiked to Salt Lake City, Utah. He talked me into taking this trip because he had hopes of finding a job there. When we arrived, we forgot about all about finding work. We stayed drunk for a whole month. I stole some money from some passed out drunk and then hitchhiked back to Cortez to see my mom. I didn't have money to buy liquor, so my friends and I went to the city park hoping to find someone who would give us some money.

"Hey, Roho! Look! There's your mom and step-dad!" my

friends yelled, pointing to a car. I took off running thinking I could catch them and accidentally ran into a young girl.

I yelled, "Sorry!" and continued running but didn't catch up with the car. I went back to the park where my friends and I combined our loose change. We had enough for a bottle of cheap wine. When that ran out, we had to find some more money. We were working on that when the police stopped us and I was arrested for assault because of my run-in with the little girl.

Trumped Up Charges

I was booked, arraigned and given a public defender because I had no money. I read the report. It said that I had followed the girl home after the alleged assault. This was not true. They must have been looking for a way to get rid of me, the unwanted, miserable, drunken Indian. They must have convinced the little girl to say things about me. I have been guilty of many things in my life, but this time I was not guilty. I would never hurt a child in any way.

The judge ordered me to check in at the state mental hospital in Pueblo, Colorado for an evaluation. I was there for two weeks before I even saw a doctor. This was a very frightening time for me. I knew not mentally ill. I was an alcoholic and a drug addict—not crazy!

Not Crazy, Just Addicted

I saw patients who looked like zombies. I was afraid that I would become like them and thought I might never get released. I told the nurses I wanted to go home, so they assigned me janitorial duties to keep me busy. When the doctor finally did see me, his evaluation consisted of me counting backwards from one hundred, which I did with no problem. He said, "You are not crazy. I'll call the sheriff to come get you."

I was finally released from the mental hospital, I was sent back to Cortez where I met with my public defender. He told me he believed we could beat the assault charge. I was relieved. After all,

I was innocent and I didn't want people to think otherwise.

Cheating Death, Again

I was out on bail and going back and forth from Cortez to Farmington when something very strange happened. I was drinking with friends and ended up passed out by a gulch. Apparently, some teens saw me and threw me face down into the creek. I was unaware of what was going on, until I heard a voice saying in Navajo, "Don't breathe. Don't breathe!"

I came up out of the water. I saw teenagers running away and figured out what had happened. All of a sudden, I was no longer under the influence of alcohol. I believe with all my heart that if I had not heard the voice telling me not to breathe, I would have drowned that day. The Lord did not want me to surrender to an early death.

This incident and that voice are forever embedded into my memory. Even though I didn't know who or what it was at the time, God had intervened in my hopeless life several times. The first time was when I almost froze to death in the creek bed when the police were searching for me after robbing a gas station. The second time was when the angel stroked my hair in Farmington. The third time was when I was about to freeze to death and I saw fire jumping. When I heard the voice saying, "Don't breathe. Don't breathe," I should have recognized the feeling and responded to the Lord, but I didn't.

I now consider the overwhelming baptism of love I felt on these special occasions evidence of God's great grace and mercy. For reasons I did not understand at the time, my death was put off many times. Even though I was reckless and had stopped caring about my life, God never stopped caring. His watchful eye was on me the whole time I was out of control.

We'll Pay You to Leave Our State

In the meantime, I was told it would be better if I left Colorado. A man worked up a plan to send me to a Christian rehab program in California. Just before my court appearance, my public defender (from the assault case) backed down from his original belief about beating the charge. He now believed I would be convicted, so I decided to plead guilty.

This time I was willing to be the victim. By pleading guilty, I received a deferred sentence of three years. The public defender and the prosecutor both recognized that going to trial would be costly. They wanted to get rid of me and cut expenses.

Everyone involved knew I wasn't guilty, but they wanted me out of Cortez. So the judge gave me $100.00. The public defender and prosecutor also threw in a couple hundred dollars. The money was to be used for a bus ticket for my new beginning in California

That was how badly they wanted me out of Colorado.

TRANSITIONS

 *Wil*

For there is one God and one Mediator between God and men, the Man Christ Jesus...

1 Timothy 2:5

*"My name is Wil Yazzie
and I am a social worker."*

The assault charge from Colorado was dismissed when I agreed to check into a rehabilitation facility in the Los Angeles area. My mom and step-dad took me to the bus depot in Cortez so I could begin my new life in California. Something told me I'd never see my mom again. I looked at her and said, "I love you, Mom." I shook my step-dad's hand and said, "Take care of Mom." I was right. That was the last time I ever saw my mother alive.

I arrived in California in 1988 an angry man. I was thankful my sentence had been changed from incarceration to rehabilitation, but I was still furious that someone was able to add a trumped up charge onto my record.

Christian Rehab verses Native Rehab

I checked into a Christian rehab facility in Hawthorne, California called Victory Outreach. I was in rehab for four and half months, but I had trouble adjusting. It was a strict faith-based program and I could not accept their ways. My anger kept breaking through and that led to fights with fellow residents. Also, I was the only Native American in the program. I felt isolated so I got drunk one day and left the program.

I went to downtown Los Angeles and found the United American Indian Involvement, Inc., a community based non-profit formed to serve Native Americans in Los Angeles county. I wanted to try their recovery program. I told a case manger I had just left a Christian rehab place. The UAII program was based on traditional beliefs. They sent me to Long Beach where I became a resident of the Eagle Lodge. The Eagle Lodge was based on The Red Road, a healing phrase used by many different Native American tribal communities.

The Red Road and Vision Quests

The Red Road represents one who is walking the road of balance, living right and following the rules of the Creator. I became very involved in traditional beliefs and started going to pow-wows and sweat lodges every week. The leader of the sweat lodge approached me and said, "Wil, you have all this education—you can help people. Fight the enemy with your education."

He and several others encouraged me to go on a vision quest. I was supposed to think about how I could become a warrior for my people. A seed was planted in my mind that if I could help myself, I also could help others. I thought I had found the answer to my problems.

Outwardly, I appeared to be a different person, but on the inside, I was still full of the same anger and addictive traits that had destroyed my life. I was a sinner without hope—trying to change my life through man-made traditions. That never works.

My Life Begins to Take Shape

I wasn't penalized for breaking my probabtion when I left Victory Outreach because the Eagle Lodge wrote a letter to the court stating I was in their recovery program. After I completed the program, I went to a halfway house. I had to find work within two weeks or I would be asked to leave the house. Thankfully, I found a job with a Christian social service center as an employment specialist.

I went back to Cortez when my Mom passed away in 1989. I saw her at the funeral home but did not stay for the funeral. My brothers and sisters were heavy drinkers, so I helped my step-dad pay for funeral expenses and then returned to Long Beach where there would be less drinking.

At the time, I was dating Jo Ann, my boss at the Christian social services center. On September 8, 1989, Jo Ann and I got married. I was no longer lonely or in need of a permanent home. My life was beginning to take shape.

In order to complete my degree in social work, I took classes at California State University in Long Beach. I transfered these few remaining credits to the University of Cincinnati and got my degree. During this time, I quit my job as the employment specialist and got another job with the newly established Department of Mental Health of Los Angeles county. Then, while I was working for the Department of Mental Health, I got a call from the Long Beach Mental Health Services. They wanted me to work for them. Jo Ann and I lived in Long Beach, so I took the job and worked there for two years.

An Experienced Role Model

Even though there were many Native Americans living and struggling in Long Beach, there were no Native American programs. Homelessness, drugs, unemployment and alcoholism were rampant. Our neighborhood had challenging problems. Native Americans with disabilities received no support. Native kids were joining gangs and forgetting about their culture. Help was desperately needed, but no one had a plan or a solution.

I offered to start my own program called the Four Feathers American Indian Program. I was able to get funding from private donations and the United Methodist Church. For the first time in my life, I felt as if I was living up to my potential and helping others. People looked up to me. Once again, I was a gang leader, but this time I was an experienced role model with a plan. My criminal past was seen as positive motivation for the people I worked with.

"Don't drink or do drugs," I told the young people. "Don't waste your life like I did."

I helped Native kids get involved in pow-wows and taught them to embrace their heritage. At the time, I did not realize that some of my advice was not sound.

Chapter Thirty-One

ACTING IS AN ART

But we are all like an unclean thing, and all our righteousnesses are like filthy rags; we all fade as a leaf, and our iniquities, like the wind, have taken us away.

Isaiah 64:6

It never occurred to Wil that he might have genuine artistic abilities until one day when he got a call from the Southwest Museum in Los Angeles. They invited Wil to attend an upcoming workshop they were sponsoring for Native American actors. It was 1994. When he arrived, he did not know anybody. However, when he saw actress Jane Seymour, he introduced himself.

Good Advice from Ms. Jane Seymour

Ms. Seymour was interested to learn Wil was a social worker, so he told her about his Four Feathers program. After a good half hour conversation, he decided to ask her a specific question. "How do I get involved in acting?" he asked her.

"Come with me," the actress said. "I'll introduce you to some people who can help you."

Wil met Larry Sellers, the actor who portrayed Cloud Dancing in Seymour's show, *Dr. Quinn, Medicine Woman*. Ms. Seymour also made sure he met other Native American actors and Hollywood notables. Wil enjoyed meeting people involved in the arts. With such a grand introduction to Hollywood, Wil began to see acting as an art form he could become passionate about. He realized he wanted to join this interesting community of accomplished people.

First Hollywood Gigs

His new friends talked to him about acting classes, headshots, how to get an agent, and most importantly, how to succeed in Hollywood. "You need to do this, then that..." They took him through the process step by step. He must have made a great first impression because one week later, someone called him who was working on a movie called *Sioux City*, a film directed by and starring Lou Diamond.

"Would you like to get involved?" he asked Wil.

Ah, ya-esssss! In Navaho, that would be aoo'!

Wil was cast as the featured drummer character in the film, *Sioux City*. This is when he discovered he was not shy in front of cameras. The man who was normally reserved (unless fighting or leading fellow gang members in crimes against society) had suddenly caught the acting bug. Wil very much enjoyed being in the spotlight.

Calls for extras (background actors) were routinely publicized in L.A., which was one of the recommended stepping stones mentioned to Wil for breaking into Hollywood as a new actor. Wil wanted to get a part in an action-adventure film directed by and starring Steven Segal called *On Deadly Ground*. Wil knew he had the complete Native look—the handmade turquoise jewelry, a well-worn hat, and impressive snakeskin boots, which is why he confronted the famous actor and said, "I want to be in your movie."

"Book him," Seagal told his people, a phrase Wil had heard many times before, only this time it meant put him on the payroll, not put him in jail.

His determination paid off. He was featured as a tribal representative and appeared in the courtroom scenes. He was off to a good start. He needed one more speaking part to qualify for membership in SAG (Screen Actor's Guild), so Wil went to audition for a part in the television show, *Star Trek—The Next Generation*. The casting director was looking for a Native American with a special look, for an episode called "The Long Journey." Wil was last person they auditioned. He got the part.

No, No, No—Poof, You're a SAG Actor

Wil played the part of a protesting elder. In the story, he and his people did not want to relocate to another planet. He had only one line: "No," but he said it three times, and that somehow met the guild's membership requirements. A trinity of refusals is all it took to establish Wil's professional acting credentials.

Wil started working with an agent and a manager, just as his colleagues had advised. He was determined to take acting seriously, but he was still managing his Four Feathers program. Then, an unexpected path in politics opened up for Wil that fed his escalating desire to help his people.

And a Lobbyist for Native Americans

Wil and a group from the Native American Indian Commission of Los Angeles County traveled to Washington, D.C. where they were scheduled to speak to White House officials about the U.S. – Navajo Treaty of 1868. Although they had high hopes of meeting with President Clinton, they did not get to meet the Commander in Chief. They did, however, get the opportunity to encourage high-ranking government officials to remember and uphold the pledges our government made to help Native people with regard to medical, education and housing needs.

At the time, sixty percent of Native people were living in urban areas and getting no government assistance. All government financial aid went to Indians living on reservations; none of it went to those who left the reservation. The small but ambitious group proved to be an effective agent in getting help for urban Native Americans.

Wil had done what he set out to do. He was elated knowing that he had significantly influenced lawmakers to the point where the lives of Navajo people across United States of America would be greatly improved. While walking through the hallways of our nation's capital, Wil realized he had become a successful lobbyist. Never in his wildest dreams did he imagine he would become a Native American delegate advocating on behalf of his people in this fashion. In a very real sense, he had become a true Navajo warrior.

While running the Four Feathers program, Wil also discovered disabled Native Americans had to deal with unemployment and other social issues without aid from the government. For this reason and in conjunction with the California Rehabilitation Social Services Agency, he founded a program for disabled Native Americans in Downey, California. Eventually, Wil relieved himself of his duties at Four Feathers.

Surface Success

On the surface, Wil finally appeared to be in the early stages of a very successful life, but on the inside, he was still unchanged, and like a teakettle boiling, his life was building up pressure and he was about to explode. Wil believed The Red Road had changed him, but the enemy of his soul had deceived him once more. While Wil's Eagle Lodge experience may have planted ideas that later produced positive outcomes, it did not solve his addiction problem.

From 1989 through 1994, Wil did very well. He was under the impression his addictions were finally under control. He was totally immersed in Native traditional ways and thought that he had found the key to success as a person. However, he was about to discover an ugly truth. He was still an alcoholic and serving the wrong master.

Garlic Breath Triggers the Binge Drinker in Wil

Wil was invited to a reception to honor the Native American Man of the Year, an accolade he dreamed of achieving one day. The meal was an Italian dish loaded with garlic, so the next morning, Jo Ann tactfully suggested he use mouthwash to get rid of his garlic breath. Wil used a mouth rinse that contained alcohol and accidentally swallowed some. One swig was all it took to throw Wil back into the arms of alcohol. He went on a two-week binge, forgetting about his programs, his marriage and his dreams. Once again, Wil didn't care about anything but getting his next drink.

Because Wil did not return to work, his social programs dissolved, which made him miserable and led to another binge, only this one lasted two months. He ended up on skid row in downtown Los Angeles, sleeping in cardboard boxes or on the street. He went from social activist to bum. And to think Italian cuisine and mouthwash were to blame.

Last Rites for the Unfortunate Hobo

One night, when Wil was roaming the streets of downtown Long Beach, he began to vomit blood. He called Jo Ann and asked her to come pick him up. She called 911 instead. While the hospital doctors worked on him, a priest came by and asked if he could pray for "the poor man." Wil did not realize that the doctors had given up on trying to stop his acute hemorrhaging, or that the priest was there to give him last rites. Wil told the priest he was not Catholic but a traditionalist. Before leaving the emergency room, the holy man managed to squeeze in a prayer for the unfortunate hobo.

Wil remembers hearing a doctor say, "I am going to try one

more procedure." He woke up the next morning and immediately realized he had cheated death. Once again, death was put off.

Jo Ann allowed Wil to return home. While he renounced drinking, Jo Ann was about to renounce Wil. His second marriage, battered by alcohol, was on the verge of being terminated. Any minor marital problems Jo Ann and Wil might have had were intensified when Wil drank. The only recourse, in Wil's mind, was to go back to The Red Road.

Rebounding on the Red Road

After completing a second round of traditional rehab, Wil was motivated to start a program for at-risk youth in Lynwood, California. Gangs, drugs, homelessness and alcohol were huge problems for Native American youth. His expertise was greatly needed and appreciated. He did not like seeing young people becoming involved in the gang culture. His goal was to help young people before they ended up in prison. As he did before, he started a community program and gave it one hundred percent of his energy.

Feeling as if his life was getting back on the right track, Wil decided to take professional acting classes. With help from an agent, he scoured the entertainment listings and was awarded parts in television, movies, theater and commercials and became a member of both SAG and AFTRA (American Federation of Television and Radio Artists). Wil also enjoyed performing on stage. The applause of a live audience offered the instant gratification he craved.

Divorced but Still Married to the Bottle

Despite many positive developments in his career and personal life, Wil could not resist the urge to drink. He got drunk one day and decided he could no longer stand to be married. He left his second wife so he could drink without criticism. Once the proud owner two beautiful homes, Wil left his prosperous and productive life to take up the life of a bum.

It's almost impossible to believe he went back to living on the streets, and that by choosing alcohol, he was also choosing homelessness. Sadly, the man who had come so far had fallen even lower than even he could have imagined. This particular homeless spell lasted two years.

A hopeless alcoholic living on the streets of Long Beach assembling meals from dumpsters—Wil Yazzie had become a fugitive from his own life.

Wil got off the streets in 1998 when he returned Newcomb, New Mexico to help care for his Dad. His father, though his health was not good, was still herding sheep and caring for his wife. Wil got a job as a counselor working with abused women and children to support himself and help his family. Ironically, he was counseling abusive husbands who were causing the women and children in their lives to suffer unnecessary (and often excessive) hardship.

The following year the Navajo Nation hired him to be a social worker. At the same time, he was awarded a couple of parts in movies produced by the Four Directions health program. He also conducted acting classes in Shiprock. He went to sweat lodge ceremonies and participated in pow-wows where he danced, chanted and drummed. Life was at least manageable.

Then Wil's father had a stroke and never recovered. He was in a nursing home until his death in 2001. After his dad's death, Wil decided to go back to California and pursue life as an urban Native. He missed the excitement of Los Angeles. Since the Navajo Nation had granted him a divorce, he was free to pursue his interests without the distraction of an inconvenient marital attachment. On the other hand, his interest in alcohol had not yet been severed. He was still married to the bottle.

Chapter Thirty-Two

LAST CHANCE

 *Wil*

Therefore, if anyone is in Christ, he is a new creation; old things have passed away; behold, all things have become new.

2 Corinthians 5:17

*"My name is Wil Yazzie
and I am a born again Christian, FINALLY!"*

After my father's death, I went to California and got a job with United American Indian Involvement. Once again, I was assigned to work with addicts as a counselor. I counseled Natives to keep on The Red Road and encouraged them to embrace Native American spirituality. I spoke about The Great Spirit, The Great Mystery, Grandfather and God but never mentioned Jesus Christ. I also talked about how sweat lodges and dancing at pow-wows helped me.

However, I was wrong.

Temporary Band-Aids

These things were temporary band-aids. I did not tell them that once the band-aid came off, I continually returned to my addictions.

I had opportunities to build my acting career. I wanted to be a good actor and an example to the youth. I thought that if they saw me on television, they might want to follow in my footsteps, or at least do something positive with their lives. My goal in becoming an actor was to inspire others to do good things.

Life was beginning to look and feel pretty good again. It was 2004, and I started to believe I was healed from all my problems. I was living in downtown Los Angeles for a while, but when my brother lost his home, we moved to Long Beach and got an apartment together. Everything was going well, and then one of my neighbors gave me a beer. I thought I could drink socially. Of course, that never works for an alcoholic. That one beer set me off into a month long binge.

Given In to Alcholism

I was driving in a blackout one night and woke up the next morning in a hospital. I had no idea what had happened. I found later out that I had wrecked my car. I was out of control. I knew I had hit rock bottom, so I resigned from my counseling job before they fired me. Even though I went through several more rehab programs, I relapsed, just like my many previous attempts at sobriety.

Using the excuse that a change of scenery would help me, I went to Indianapolis to visit one of my brothers. It was not a good visit. He stayed drunk the entire time I was there. The situation was getting volatile, so I decided to leave. I bought a used car and drove back to California.

Before leaving Indianapolis, I thought about calling or visiting Linda, but I knew I was still dealing with a lot of issues. I didn't want to risk hurting her again. Plus, I wasn't sure what her reaction would be if I called her. I didn't know if she was still single or if she had remarried. In the end, I decided not to contact her. I believe God was protecting Linda. He knew I was not ready to turn my life over to Him.

When I got back to California, I moved into a cheaper apartment in Downey. I thought that moving to a new place apart from my brother would help my situation. I was sober for about three months and then a friend gave me some heroin. Trying a small amount of heroin set me off to drinking—again!

Diabetes

During this time, I found out I was diabetic. I was supposed to be on insulin and controlling my diet. Instead, I started drinking a very sweet brand of liquor. It didn't take long before I couldn't get up and walk. A neighbor found me rolling around on the floor and called 911. When the medical personnel took my blood pressure, the doctor told me he was amazed that I did not have a stroke or heart attack. He said my blood glucose levels were so high that if I had delayed in getting help for another half hour, I could have had a stroke or heart attack, and mostly likely, I would have died.

Again, the Lord spared my life, but why? I did not know. Now I know that people were praying for me even though they did not know where I was or what I was doing. I wonder if this was one of the times when they were down on their knees.

I left Downey and returned to my brother's place in Long Beach. My brother didn't hide the fact he was unhappy about me sleeping on his couch. But since I paid my share of the rent and paid for food from residual checks I had received from acting jobs, he let me stay. My driver's license had been revoked when I wrecked my car, so I decided to sell the car I had bought in Indianapolis (as well as another car I had stolen), which left me with a few dollars and absolutely no earthly possessions—again!

Hitting Rock Bottom

I was very upset about hitting rock bottom. Believe it or not, I celebrated by getting drunk. It was New Year's Eve, 2004. For some reason, I began to think about how many times my life had been spared from certain death. I recognized that the Lord had saved my life and delivered me from many disasters. And it dawned on me that Satan was too powerful and alcohol was his leash. I knew my problems would never go away if I continued to believe Satan's lies.

The enemy of God wanted my life to end, but God wanted me to live. Finally, and I mean finally, my eyes were wide open. I could see my enemy and it was time to face him. If the Lord was fighting for me (and apparently He was), then it was time to switch sides. I no longer wanted to play for the enemy's team. It was New Year's Day, 2005 and the day I took my last alcoholic drink.

Could Not Shake The Feeling

For the first time in my life, I saw myself as I really was—a sinner. Without Jesus Christ, there was no hope for me to ever get it right. Somehow, I knew this was my last chance and that if I turned away from God at this point, all hope would be lost. I had no doubt I would die from alcohol abuse the very next time I got drunk. I couldn't shake the feeling that God would not save me as He had so many times before.

One day, as I was looking for work and praying to God for help, I cried out, "Please help me, Jesus!" I remembered my life in Cincinnati and realized that my days of playing games with the Lord were over. I made the decision to repent and turn my entire life over to Jesus Christ. I didn't feel any profound excitement, but I knew for certain I belonged to Jesus Christ. The tug of war was finally over when I finally surrendered.

My life did not change for the better right away. I was still unemployed and walking the streets looking for work. However, I was a new person on the inside. My spirit became alive to God through his son, Jesus Christ. I experienced a second birth. Jesus took away my desire for alcohol and drugs. My deliverance was real, but I also had to stay away from bad influences. I had stopped serving the enemy and he was not happy. At times, he tried to make it difficult for me to serve God, but I recognized and resisted his temptations.

Prior to my conversion to true Christianity, I had a foul mouth. Because of the years I had spent in prison and on the streets, bad language, dirty jokes and cussing had become my normal way of speaking. Every other word was an obscenity or blasphemy against God. But the Lord reached into my heart and performed a miracle. Without any effort on my part, I gave up using foul language.

Looking for Work and God

My economic situation did not change immediately. The Lord was testing me while growing my faith in Him. I was determined to not give up, even if my faith was the size of a mustard seed. As I walked around town looking for work, I prayed. The small pocket Bible I carried around was my constant and physical reminder of my new life in Christ.

I went to temporary employment agencies but did not receive any job offers. When it came to applying for a position in social work, I was told I had to be bilingual—as in they wanted me to speak English and Spanish. This was very upsetting because I was bilingual, only I spoke Navajo and English. I was reminded of the many times at boarding school when I had been punished for speaking Navajo. It would have been easy for me to slip into bitterness. But because I had filled my mind with scripture verses, there was no room for the enemy's lies. I recognized bitterness as one of the tools Satan would use to discourage me, so I rejected any thought or feeling that did not agree with the Bible.

There were times when I felt like giving up and thought about going back to drinking, but I prayed that the Lord would keep me close to Him. I found Bible stories that showed how God intervenes when one of his children is about to fall. Reading those stories kept me strong in my faith. I believed something good would come out of my time of trial. I didn't want to give up. I wanted to hang on.

I looked for work for several long months. As I searched for employment, I also talked with the Lord. For the first time in decades, I was not feeding my addictions or covering them up. And because of that, the world looked and felt completely different.

Chapter Thirty-Three

ALL THESE THINGS

 *Wil*

But seek first the kingdom of God and His righteousness, and all these things shall be added to you.

Matthew 6:33

"My name is Wil Yazzie
and I am totally pardoned."

One day I went to the library to check my e-mail for job offers. Over time, I had lost interest in social networking sites, but since I didn't have much of a schedule, I decided to check my account. I saw a message from someone named Nancy and thought it was from a photographer friend of mine.

I opened it and was shocked to find out it was from Linda's sister, my former sister-in-law. I wrote her back and asked if I could write to Linda. I told Nancy I wanted to apologize for all the pain I had caused her sister.

Twenty-Eight Years Later

It had been twenty-eight years since Linda and I had last seen each other. I still loved her. As a new Christian, I knew I needed to make an effort to make things better between us. Nancy agreed and gave me Linda's e-mail address. On September 26, 2008, I wrote to Linda and asked her to forgive me. It was the hardest letter I've ever written. I didn't know if she would write back or not. I certainly wouldn't have blamed her if she didn't.

The next day I went to the library to check my email and there was a message from Linda. I was nervous when I opened it. In her email, she told me that she had forgiven me the day I left her. She also said she held no bitterness in her heart toward me. I was happy to hear she had become an ordained minister, but not all of her news was good. Some parts of her letter were sad. She said that her older sister Frankie and her mother had both passed away. The pastor who married us had also died earlier that year.

We started writing to each other every day. Emails turned into phone calls. We had a lot of catching up to do, so our conversation would sometimes last three hours or more. Both of us confessed that we had never stopped loving each other. Linda told me she had never stopped praying for me. Although it sounds impossbile, the woman I deserted prayed for me for nearly three decades.

Will You Marry Me, Again?

One night in October, I brought up the subject of one day, remarrying. She told me she was not ready to make a commitment right then but said she would pray about it. A few hours later, my phone rang. It was Linda. "Yes," Linda said. "I'll remarry you." We decided we should remarry as soon as possible because so many years had gone by.

I traveled to Cincinnati by train. It was 3:45 in the morning on November 12th, 2008 when I arrived. Linda and her sister, Nancy, and her husband, Steve, were waiting for me at Cincinnati's Union Terminal. All the way there, I kept wondering how Linda and I would act when we first saw each other. I entered the lobby and saw Linda with her arms wide open, reaching for me. We embraced. We were so happy to be in one another's arms. We hugged, and it was as if nothing bad had happened between us. How could twenty-eight years simply melt away? I can only say that God's great love created this miraculous moment.

The mayor of Lockland, Ohio performed our second wedding ceremony at City Hall ten days later. We honeymooned at the Great Wolf Lodge outside Cincinnati. We were so happy, and in many ways, happier than we were at our first wedding. We had both been through so much. I never imagined that Linda and I would be reunited as man and wife—not after all I put her through. This time I knew our marriage would have a strong foundation. I was no longer the self-centered person who thought he could do it all on his own. I no longer thought about my "buddies" in Farmington. Jesus Christ would be the head of our home. I was ready to forsake all others and be responsible for Linda's well being.

Our Calling to Minister

As we talked, it became obvious to both of us that God had repeatedly spared my life. This is why Linda and I made a commitment to serve Him for the rest of our lives—and we would do it together. We became active in our Lockland Church of the Nazarene. We sang in the choir and co-taught a Sunday school class. We also started a recovery program called *Christ Is The Answer*, or *C.I.T.A.* The program ministers to people struggling with addiction. Because of our combined backgrounds, we were also able to help family members who had loved ones struggling with addiction.

God blessed our efforts and the *C.I.T.A.* program began to grow, which is why I thought we would spend the rest of our lives serving the Lord in Cincinnati. But one day Linda approached me with a new idea. She felt that the Lord was calling us to minister on the Navajo Nation reservation. She thought the Lord wanted us to tell our story to my fellow Native American people.

At first, I was undecided. I thought it would be hard for Linda to adapt to life on the reservation. I knew she would face certain cultural and language barriers. Even though Linda's health had improved since our first marriage, I worried that life on the reservation would be too much for her. But I promised I would pray about it, and soon the Holy Spirit began to deal with me about our calling. I remembered how I had ignored God's leading and suffered needlessly for over half of my life. This time I would not ignore God.

Moving to the reservation required a lot of preparation. Linda had purchased the Amyx family home after her mother died and gone back to work at Lockland Elementary School, even though she had retired after working there for thirty years. We were established and happy with the way things were, yet we decided to step out in faith. We decided we would make the move to the reservation without support from any organization or ministry.

We took a trip to the reservation in April 2010 to see if we could buy a home there. Nothing seemed to work out, so we returned to Ohio. We prayed and put everything in the Lord's hands. We planned to move on the first of June even though we had no idea where we were going to live. If God called us, as we believed He had, we believed He would provide a place and work out all the details.

The Amyx family home sold very quickly. With the real estate market in such a slump, there was no equity left in the home. Although Linda did not make a profit, we were pleased. We were free to make our move out west. We purchased a modest mobile home for a reasonable price over the phone, but we still had to figure out where we were going to live. We finally realized that the Lord wanted us to live on my dad's homesite in Newcomb, New Mexico.

Together and In Ministry

Linda's last day of work was Wednesday, May 28th, 2008. After she said good-bye to her friends and colleagues, we went to the settlement meeting for the Amyx home, packed our personal possessions and four dogs into my pickup truck, and headed for New Mexico. We were together and we were in ministry!

Living Proof

I know what a burden feels like whether it comes from rejection, bitterness, loneliness, homelessness, or sexual or substance abuse. No matter how low a person has sunk, or how deep of a pit someone has to climb out of (or feels trapped in), I can identify. I am living proof Jesus loves all people no matter what they've done or how long they've sinned. Linda and I are living proof that severely damaged relationships can be restored. And that is why we were so determined to move. We knew we could do the most good on the reservation.

Whether I'm on the reservation or off, I tell people not to make the mistake of playing games with God like I did. There is a popular belief in the world today that says it doesn't matter what you believe as long as you are sincere. People believe all is well because all religions lead to God, and that is a lie from the pit of hell. God tells us there is only ONE WAY, and we must come to Him through His son, Jesus Christ. No religious or traditional program can save you. We all have eternal life given to us by our Creator, and we will spend it either in heaven or hell.

For an alcoholic like me, or for anyone who has lived without hope like I did, there is nothing more beautiful than the truth found in **2 Corinthians 5:17**: *"If anyone is in Christ, he is a new creation; the old things have gone, the new has come!"*

Chapter Thirty-Four

TOTAL FORGIVENESS

 *Linda*

But Jesus looked at them and said, "With men it is impossible, but not with God; for with God all things are possible."

Mark 10:27

"My name is Linda Yazzie and I am living my dream, and serving the Lord with my husband, Wil!"

When Wil and I reunited in 2008, it was as if we had never been apart. It was like, "Hi, honey. Where've you been?" There was no anxiety or awkwardness or rehashing of the past. Neither one of us felt self-conscious. We simply picked up where we left off as if he had only been gone for a short while. It was truly amazing!

Letting Go of Our Past

I can honestly say the Lord supernaturally healed all the bad memories between us. The way we overlooked our past reminded me of book *The Hiding Place*, a story written by Corrie Ten Boom. Ms. Ten Boon, a Christian author, wrote about how Holocaust survivors were miraculously able to overlook the horrors they had faced while trapped in Nazi concentration camps. Any recollection of our struggles was like that—mysteriously passed over.

In all the years he was gone, I never thought about the bad things that happened in our marriage. Wil was always very sweet to me and this is what was made our separation so difficult. Our good memories were kept alive through faith and prayer. You can imagine how excited I was to get an email from Wil. And to think we have Facebook to thank for our reunion!

I Forgave Him the Day He Left

Right from the start, Wil apologized for all the pain he had caused my family and me. I wrote back immediately. I wanted him to know that I forgave him the day he left. As a Christian, I could not hold bitterness in my heart or have hard feelings toward anyone for any reason. I told Wil I had given everything over to the Lord and that I had been praying for him continually throughout the years. We started talking on the phone, and like before, we had so much to talk about.

Then one night he asked, "Do you think it's possible we could remarry?" I didn't give him an answer right away. I wanted to pray about it first. It was around midnight when I called him back and said, "I would LOVE to get remarried!!!"

Here's the thing. Wil and I love each other so much. I cannot thank the Lord enough for restoring our marriage and bringing Wil back to me. I try to tell at least one person every day about how the Lord honors and rewards us when we put our faith and trust in Him.

We knew God had brought us back together for good reason. It didn't take long to figure out that the Lord wanted us to lead a Christian recovery program.

Christ Is The Answer, Recovery Program

People responded whenever and wherever Wil gave his testimony. With this kind of response, we felt led to establish a ministry called *Christ Is The Answer (C.I.T.A.)*. Wil's recovery program, which was later modified to fit the practical needs of Native Americans, could accommodate smaller groups and one-on-one ministry. It proved to be effective. Lives were changed as people came to trust in Christ for their recovery.

Both of us assumed we'd live in Cincinnati the rest of our lives, but at the same time, I felt the Lord calling us into ministry on the reservation. After much prayer, Wil and I made the decision to leave Ohio. We were in complete agreement and could not ignore God's calling to serve Navajo people.

We arrived in Gallup, New Mexico on June 1, 2010, eager set up housekeeping in our mobile home on the Yazzie's leased land in nearby Newcomb. Even though the home was delivered the next day, we had to stay at our motel in Gallup for a week before our electric and water was turned on. It took a few weeks before we were able to buy furniture, but we were so happy to be together and living in New Mexico.

Getting Involved

We wanted to get involved in a church right away. A friend of Wil's was the pastor at an Assembly of God church in Shiprock, so we decided to go there. Pastor Bill was a friend to Wil when he was in prison and had prayed for Wil many times throughout the years. Pastor Bill spoke English and Navajo and his wife was Anglo, like me. We loved Pastor Bill's church and the people there but the long drive into Shiprock kept us from getting involved in church activities, which is why it was hard for us to leave and look for another church. Fortunately, there was an Assembly of God church in Newcomb, so we decided to become part of that congregation.

Giving Up Traditional Beleifs and Practices

Some people may find this part of our story a little difficult to accept but it is an important part of who we are today. Wil and I had gone to pow-wows in the tri-state area when we lived in Cincinnati. The events were mostly social gatherings attended by admirers of Native American cultures. When we attended pow-wows in the southwest, we discovered they were quite different from the ones we had been attending in Ohio.

One day when Wil was performing in a pow-wow as a Gourd Dancer, the Holy Spirit spoke to him and said, "Leave right now!" I was sitting on the sidelines when he came over and told me that the Holy Spirit wanted him to leave. We wanted to please the Lord in every area of our lives, so we left and never went back.

Wil's sudden and overwhelming conviction made me realize that if we wanted to continue to walk in God's light, Wil must give up anything that involved witchcraft, including dancing and chanting at pow-wows. We couldn't involve ourselves in events where spirits were literally being summoned. The scripture that came to mind was: *"Therefore come out from them and be separate, says the Lord. Touch no unclean thing, and I will receive you."* (2 Corinthians 6:17)

People may not realize that many Navajo traditional beliefs are basically witchcraft. Consequently, traditionalists in the Navajo Nation can find themselves bound by Satan and held captive by superstitions and fears. Many Navajos are afraid of various animals and make decisions based on taboos that have been passed down from generation to generation. For example, Wil has seen a skinwalker and lived to tell about it. He crossed where "the snake has crawled" and yet his body is not crooked.

Invading the Enemy's Territory

Satan is real and so are skinwalkers experienced in traditionalist beliefs—except they are supernatural demonic manifestations. Ceremonies and superstitious beliefs had opened doors in Wil's life that weren't good. We could no longer ignore such an important fact. Taboos that sound more like curses than instruction say things like "If you do ...., then .... will happen." These are man's traditions that promote the enemy's lies.

We presented a plan before the church board at Newcomb to restart our ministry, *Christ Is The Answer.* We were very excited when it was approved and incorporated by the Navajo Nation. I was thrilled knowing my dream of becoming a minister's wife was coming true. Alcohol, drugs, domestic violence, child abuse, unemployment, and homelessness are epidemic here, perhaps more than anywhere else in the United States.

Wil and I knew we were invading enemy territory. As Chrisitan ministers, we affect people whose families had been held captive for many generations. Wil and I consider it a great honor to be called by God to bring the light and beauty of His mercy to spiritually dark places.

Since moving to the reservation, we've learned firsthand how widespread Native suicides are, especially among the youth. Wil and I see so many young people dressed in black, gothic-type clothing with skulls and other symbols of death on them, and we are grieved. Clearly, we are deeply involved in spiritual warfare. However, to fight the battle, we have no need for corn pollen or eagle feathers. We put on the whole armor of God and come equipped with the truth.

Jesus said to him, "I am the way, the truth, and the life. No one comes to the Father except through Me. **John 14:6**

Then Jesus said to those Jews who believed Him, "If you abide in My word, you are My disciples indeed. 32 And you shall know the truth, and the truth shall make you free." **John 8:31–32**

Finally, my brethren, be strong in the Lord and in the power of His might. Put on the whole armor of God, that you may be able to stand against the wiles of the devil. For we do not wrestle against flesh and blood, but against principalities, against powers, against the rulers of the darkness of this age, against spiritual hosts of wickedness in the heavenly places. Therefore take up the whole armor of God, that you may be able to withstand in the evil day, and having done all, to stand.

Stand therefore, having girded your waist with truth, having put on the breastplate of righteousness, and having shod your feet with the preparation of the gospel of peace; above all, taking the shield of faith with which you will be able to quench all the fiery darts of the wicked one. And take the helmet of salvation, and the sword of the Spirit, which is the word of God. **Ephesians 6:10–17**

Chapter Thirty-Five

CHRIST IS THE ANSWER

 *Jodie*

We are shaped and fashioned by what we love.

Johann Wolfgang Von Goethe

Like other writers who have listened to hours of cassette tapes of their subjects talking, I have often revisited the Yazzie's tapes even though they've all been transcribed. The cadence and tone of Wil's Native voice vs. Linda's innocent articulations—the contrast is intriguingly noticeable and mesmerizing.

The question is, how could, or why would a squeaky clean, evangelical Christian woman from Ohio fall madly in love with a hopeless alcoholic Native American ex-con with the last known address of Skid Row, USA? Her idyllic childhood was plagued by illness, yet filled with unconditional love and support. His childhood, splintered by divorce and plagued by poverty, was fueled by superstition and filled with disappointment. Two individuals could not be more different, yet Wil Yazzie and Linda Amyx married each other not once but twice.

Linda's Formula for Persitent Faith

Linda Yazzie, in my opinion, has earned the rights to some kind of temporal patent on total pardon and here's why. She forgave her husband despite being abandoned by him for twenty-eight years, and she did it the day he left. That's just incredible. She prayed for him daily even though his actions revealed he was more committed to drinking than his marriage. That takes stamina. She accepted, ministered to and loved him even though he was a convicted criminal and repeat offender. That takes faith—a tremendous amout of persistent faith.

Working Linda's formula backwards, first and foremost, people need Jesus. Secondly, the prayers of a righteous person are powerful and effective. And lastly, forgiveness is non-negotiable if healing is to occur. Forgiveness is the most essential, magnanimous and humbling of all acts whether it is between you and another person, or you and God.

During his decades of drinking, most people did not give Wil the time of day, let alone compassionate attention. On the outside, Wil was incorrigible and unlovable. He was an Indian with a drinking problem, an eyesore in society who buried his troubled feelings with alcohol. He was simply one of many Native Americans destined to pass out on skid row and wake up in the drunk tank.

Abandoned by family, he found another. His new family, the confused but friendly clan of alcoholics and drug addicts, accepted him as long as he provided and consumed booze. He couldn't get want he wanted so he took what he could get.

Childhood Trauma, or a Lack Thereof

Officials tell us that substance abuse is symptomatic of

underlying issues. Those issues could be a chemical imbalance or an emotional disturbance stemming from painful memories, trauma or abuse. If that's the case, Wil's painful and disconnected childhood opened the door and contributed to his chronic struggles whereas Linda's stable childhood provided the opportunity to avoid alcohol altogether. His foundation crumbled early on. Her foundation taught her to forgive and pray effectively.

Wil partied; Linda prayed. Observe the contrast. Connect the dots. Before Linda Amyx became Linda Yazzie, she lived in a Christian bubble, perfectly shielded from the evil in the world. Imagine a grown woman who doesn't even know what alcohol smells like. Surrounded by loving family, Christian friends and caring neighbors, Linda did not spend decades fighting destructive demons. Instead, she developed an intimate relationship with the Lord who often prompted her to pray.

On the other hand, Wil had to fight his way through multiple layers of sin to find love. His twisted journey was never trouble-free. It took Wil forty-four years to find the courage to change and the wisdom to accept that people don't almost freeze to death twice by drinking too much soda.

Company Kept

Wil and Linda's story proves that how one comes to acquire beliefs is a matter of who one hangs out with. Simply put, traditional Navajos acquire superstitious beliefs as a result of their community ties. The ethics and habits abusers develop are directly related to the company they keep. Christian children know (and have visits with) Christ because Christ is welcome in their home, as in the case of Linda Amyx.

You don't become a drug addict or alcoholic unless you ingest drugs or drink alcohol. You don't become a Christian unless you invite Jesus to be both Lord and Savior. If it isn't personal, it isn't real. Personal experience is the most crucial component with regard to any life choice. Listening to sermons or going to church doesn't make you a Christian just like going to a sweat lodge ceremony doesn't make you a Navajo. (And in my case, learning about a culture in a classroom doesn't make you a wise visiting teacher.)

For Wil, and many Native American Christians, the question became should a person think a little less like an Indian and a little more like a Christian? Is it possible for a Native American to thrive in two worlds? Was it possible (or necessary) to reconcile cultural differences with scripture when one's culture is expressly spiritual? Surely, there had to be a place where opposing sides could meet in the middle without sacrificing one's heritage or beliefs. It took some time but the Yazzies settled the issue once and for all. They realized the promise of spiritual protection and peace they found in God's word was sufficient. Compromising traditional beliefs with Christianity never works. On this subject, God's word was extremely clear.

Rules Taught By Men

When the religious leaders of Jesus' time saw Jesus' disciples not observing the traditional ceremonial ways, they asked Jesus, *"Why don't your disciples live according to the tradition of the elders?'Jesus replied, "These people honor me with their lips but their hearts are far from me. They worship me in vain; their teachings are but rules taught by men. You have let go of the commands of God and are holding on to the traditions of men."* **Mark 7: 1-8**

The apostle Paul writes to the Colossians with regard to this as well. *See to it that no one takes you captive through hollow and deceptive philosophies, which depend on human tradition and the basic principles of this world rather than on Christ. For in Christ, all the fullness of the Diety lives in bodily form, and you have been given fullness in Christ, who is the head over every power and authority.* **Colossians 2: 8-10**

With these and other scriptures in mind, Wil and Linda read with great interest a booklet written by a former medicine man from Canada who followed the scriptural example of burning all cursed objects.

A number who had practiced sorcery brought their scrolls together and burned them publicly. **Acts 19:19** Wil and Linda did some housecleaning of their own that resulted in a bonfire.

Thankfully, they found a church led by a Navajo pastor who shared their belief that as Christians they were not to participate in pow-wows. The prohibition stemmed from the realization traditional dancing ceremonies promoted a system of darkness rather than leading people to the light of Jesus Christ. What the Yazzies deemed an innocent pastime had become an open door to unwanted spirits. They knew medicine men and their objects had power, but their power to terrorize people came from Satan.

Wil and Linda wanted no part of any kind of false worship. The only "red road" Wil was interested in promoting was the red road created by the spilled blood of Jesus Christ, the lamb of God who was sacrificed for the sins of all people. Even though every culture comes with its own set of traditional beliefs, Wil would not allow his heritage to negate the truth found in the gospel of Jesus Christ. Furthermore, Wil knew that mixing traditional beliefs with Christianity was a recipe for disaster. Wil puts it this way: "Nothing else matters today but my Lord and Savior, Jesus Christ."

Spared Death Repeatedly

From early on, the odds favoring a long life were stacked against Wil. At three years old, he could have easily died an innocent accident victim when he tumbled from his father's moving pick-up truck. A problem drinker since age fifteen, he should been a statistic in the National Institute on Alcohol Abuse and Alcoholism's report for McKinley or San Juan county. It's not even possible to count how many car wrecks or drunken brawls he outlived.

No matter how many times the enemy tried to snuff out Wil, Wil somehow managed to pop back to life. How does a reckless, blacked-out, intoxicated teenager manage to survive not one but two cases of hypothermia? A few years later, he gets arrested for selling a firearm in a bar and given an additional five years in prison, yet he served only two, and as a result, misses a deadly prison riot. Raging relatives, bullets, knives, angry fists, numerous episodes of alcohol poisoning, virulent tuberculosis—nothing could take him out of play.

Only Jesus

A small start-up ministry such as *C.I.T.A.* has the potential to reach many people in an area where so many needs go unmet. Native Americans living on the reservation need to hear from Wil that Jesus is the answer. Wil makes himself available for one-on-one counseling, and not just for alcoholics. His experience in social work allows him the opportunity to work with many people with all kinds of issues. Now that his foundation is Jesus, and only Jesus, he is eager to minister to people in need.

It's easy to conclude after reading this book that Wil is an ordained minister and the recipient of God's grace because of Linda's fervent prayers. His happy-ending story is really about the power of prayer and God's extraordinary love. Wil and Linda are completely devoted to Christ and each other, which is why it's no surprise to find out just how eager they are to share the Good News. Wil became free from addictive, compulsive and dysfunctional behaviors through Christ, and Christ alone. Freedom paved the way to peace, serenity, joy, and most importantly, a stronger personal relationship with God and his wife Linda.

Scripture teaches that we cannot have two masters. One will be loved, the other ignored. However, there's nothing that says a person can't have two sacred stories—one of continual defeat followed by a story of redemption by means of total pardon. Just ask Wil Yazzie. He couldn't have had one without the other.

TIDBITS OF PERSONAL EXPERIENCE

Jodie Randisi

To the Navajo, everything is sacred.

Because everything is sacred there are hundreds, if not thousands of Navajo taboos containing the words *"Do not___or ___."* Taboos cover everything from coyotes, wind, high places, clouds, lightening, wild animals, domestic animals, food, string games, babies and sleep. *Do not sleep with your head pointing north or you might die.* One could argue that we all have an appointment with death, but to the Navajo north is the direction of evil and dead people lie that way. Also, *Do not thank people who help at a funeral because they will be the next to die.*

Some taboos are more for the curious tourist than for serious consideration. However, if you grew up a traditional Navajo on a reservation, you would be exposed to many such beliefs, all of which come from elders and would not be disbelieved. If you were an urbanized Navajo who has lived, or is living, off the reservation, you might not give these customary beliefs any credence whatsoever, and beyond that, you might scoff at those who repeat them.

On the other hand, if you were a curious college student back in the late 1970s looking to experience a different culture, you might decide, like I did, to pursue the opportunity to be a student teacher on a Navajo Indian reservation. And in that case, you would want to know some of the more significant taboos.

Over the last century many people have attempted to help Native Americans on reservations and failed miserably. While certain individuals and groups may have had good intentions, were well trained in their field, and thought they had a good deal to offer Navajos, they lacked understanding in the ways of Diné, the Navajo word for Navajos.

Co-Worker, Not Repairman

Acknowledging and respecting a culture's taboos and beliefs makes a huge difference in the degree of success or failure achieved, not to mention the happiness of all concerned. This is the reason I made a conscious attempt at being a good Indian helper. I wanted to be a co-worker, not a repairman.

For no apparent reason I could describe then, I chose to do my student teaching on an Indian reservation and not in the inner city of Chicago or the mountains of Appalachia. I feel it's important to note that I wasn't particularly drawn to Native Americans. My selection was a random choice that, in truth, only made sense some thirty years later when I became friends with Wil Yazzie.

From the onset, Indiana University's School of Education's American Indian Reservation Project forced me to revamp my fourth grade "First Americans" social studies unit. Upon my return to conventional classrooms in the early 80's, I sought out and was given opportunities to correct off-putting stereotypical thinking regarding Navajo Indians, all of which now stemmed from personal experience, not book learning. As the special guest speaker, I shared my half-hour mini presentation with dozens of smiling elementary students and their respective teachers, after which, I received many interesting thank you notes. This one I thought was worth sharing.

Dear: Miss Lyman. I didn't no you are hafe Indian and hafe human like us. I like that picture that the Nava Jo child did. your pretty: Amy.

Do They Still Have Indians?

What an eye-opener and belly buster! I had a good laugh and took that to mean guest speakers should offer young children more time for Q & A. At any rate, in the fall of 2011, I told an eleven-year boy that I used to teach Navajo Indians. With a puzzled look on his face, he asked, "Do they still have Indians?"

Wha-at!? Oh my. I wanted to ask him, first of all, who are "they," and how come you don't know about Native Americans? But I didn't. What I really wanted to know was who was responsible for this outrageous gap in his education. Navajos are American citizens and I think their history, past and current, should be prime national curriculum.

But I do understand the lack of information. It wasn't until I was college senior, enrolled in my student teaching preparation program, that I became somewhat informed. I was told not to fuss over Navajo babies or very young children. Navajos don't like it when strangers come close to their babies, especially when the baby still has the soft spot on his head. By his attention, a stranger may "witch the child." The result will be that the child will stutter or be unable to talk. I was told to save my "itchie, gitchie, goo" baby talk for non-Navajo young'uns. I was instructed not to use the word "maybe" because there is no word in the Navajo language that describes this concept, making it difficult for Navajos to comprehend unconfirmed intentions. This taboo almost drove me crazy.

I also found out Navajo children believe in dreams. They've been taught that dreams are sacred. Teachers, especially visiting student teachers, should listen to but never analyze dreams. I was told not to ask personal questions because Navajos do not appreciate naive attempts at showing interest in them. A Navajo will tell you about himself if and when he trusts and likes you as a friend. Small talk is unnecessary, and if you don't understand this, you will be *doo ya shoda* (no good).

My cultural sensitivities intensified during my stay on the IU campus in Bloomington, to be sure. However, some parts were skimmed over rather quickly. I suppose adequate time was not allotted for delving into the educational origins on Indian reservations, or how to avoid skinwalkers. We were there to absorb what we needed for our teaching assignment. As I remember it, IU presented a one-week, condensed, crash course that everyone acknowledged would be backed up and expanded by personal experience.

In 1979 Chinle Boarding School employees worked for the BIA (Bureau of Indian Affairs), an acting agent of the Interior Department of the United States. This agency regulated every major economic decision made by Native Americans living on a reservation. The BIA determined where and how rural Native American children received an education.

When Cultures Collide

When I finally got the opportunity to test my cultural acuity in January 1979, I knew I was headed into unfamiliar territory. My destination: Chinle Boarding School, Many Farms, Arizona, located in the upland plains. I showed up in my Smurf blue, two-door VW Rabbit affectionately named Thumper. I was on a mission to live as a foreigner without leaving the United States of America.

No more mainstream, middle-of-the-road life for Jodie Lyman. Looking forward to being a full-blown member of a minority race, I wanted to know what it felt like to be an alien, and as such, I tried to steer clear of embarrassing cultural blunders.

I concocted a mental list of what not to do based on what I knew was considered hallowed in the land where I would be living. Even though I would not be there for Halloween, my professor told me, for example, never turn a pumpkin into a jack-o-lantern. Pumpkins are food, and therefore, would never be wasted on a frivolous decorative activity. Of all the winter/spring holidays, namely President's Day, Valentine's Day, and Easter, the only potential stumbling block I could foresee was Easter. No decorating Easter eggs unless they ended up in a salad, and even then, I wasn't feeling confident enough to test the sacredness of one of my springtime traditions.

I was told to expect winter temperatures in January and February, so I packed a warm coat, plenty of turtleneck sweaters and rugged boots for hiking. Chinle Boarding School is located 70 miles northwest of Canyon de Chelly State Park—pronounced *canyon d'shay*. I was not told about their robust spring dust storms until five minutes before I experienced one.

One day, in March, a thick, choke-your-throat, clog-your-eyeballs, red blanket of desert dust completely enveloped the entire community of Many Farms. I scurried around the dormitory putting wet towels under and around doors and windows trying to keep oncoming waves of crusty dust at bay. Inconvenient weather, as it turned out, was the least of my worries. Immediately upon arriving at Chinle Boarding School, I ran head first into a non-negotiable Navajo legend, one that is forever tied to one of their most important taboos. "Want to see a picture of my boyfriend before he got his hair cut?" I asked the eighth grade girls in my dorm as I hung a giant poster of a werewolf on the back of my dorm room door.

Say Hello To Superstitions

The elders at the American Indian Program at Indiana University failed to mention the Navajo superstition involving skinwalkers. Nobody told me that skinwalkers resemble werewolves. Perhaps this subject was avoided because skinwalkers are never to be talked about, let alone taught in a classroom. Hanging a poster of one in my sleeping quarters had to be one of the dumbest ideas I ever had, especially since a skinwalker had reportedly caused a horrific car accident the week before I showed up. That, in my mind, was a cultural collision.

Eventually someone explained skinwalkers and shapeshifters to me, but it's difficult to remake a first impression, especially when you're the foreigner living in a superstitious community. I found this entry in my journal dated one week after my arrival:

> *A girl came and told us about werewolves. She's never seen one but is very scared of them. They are on the reservation, she says. They wear wolves' head and fur and walk on all fours, have superhuman strength and put curses on people. Maurice says if you touch one you will die. If they get a piece of your clothing or hair and bury it, you become very sick and must have a ceremony. There have been many deaths lately and some people think the dorm might need a ceremony.*

Oh brother. The newbie do-gooder comes to town and hangs a movie poster on her dorm room door of *Yee Naaldlooshii* and now everyone on campus is on pins and needles in need of a ceremony. For a couple of days I thought I might have to send myself home.

> NOTE: In Navajo tradition, a skinwalker is a sorcerer who transforms into a werewolf, or a man who dresses as a wolf and is believed to practice witchcraft. Their wicked activities include terrorizing people by casting spells on them and grave robbing. It is said that a skinwalker can only be defeated if one can discover his or her human identity. If a traditional faith healer cannot perform a ceremony to protect people from the danger of a skinwalker, then a person should go out at night and cover his or her body with corn pollen, cedar ash, or juniper berries.

Ut-oh. How many students did I send out into the cold, dark night seeking juniper berries? Happily, it all worked out. The students in my dorm eventually figured out that I was blindsided and innocent. Instead of shunning me, I was somewhat surprised when the students eventually accepted me. I remember celebrating when some students stole my shoes. A fifth grade teacher informed me that if (or when) a Navajo liked you, he or she would tease you. Teasing is a Navajo sign of affection. I wanted nothing more than to report back to my supervisor Dr. Mahon that I had been the recipient of a practical joke.

These are just a few of my BIA boarding school stories. Here's a look at how this system came into being, even though it reveals a disappointing and ugly side of our American government.

Dealing with the So-Called Indian Problem Through Education

Unfortunately, for the tens of thousands of Indians who went to boarding schools, it's largely remembered as a time of abuse and desecration of culture. Obviously not all American Indians had negative experiences at boarding schools. Some have fond memories of meeting spouses and making lifelong friends. Historically, however, the Navajo Nation resisted compulsory education, including boarding schools, and here's why.

Boarding schools established on Indian reservations followed the example of founder and superintendent of the Carlisle Indian Industrial School in Carlisle, Pennsylvania, General Richard Henry Pratt. Pratt was under the impression that providing vocational training while systematically stripping away tribal culture was constructive. These schools insisted students drop their Indian names, cut off their long hair, and forbade the speaking of native languages. Not surprisingly, such schools often met fierce resistance from Native Americans parents and youth. But some Indian young people responded positively, or at least ambivalently. General Pratt described his philosophy in a speech he gave in 1892.

"A great general has said that the only good Indian is a dead one," Pratt said. "In a sense, I agree with the sentiment, but only in this: that all the Indian there is in the race should be dead. Kill the Indian in him, and save the man." This is not an honorable foundation upon which to build an educational system.

Mandatory education for Indian children became law in 1893 and continued until 1978. Agents on reservations received instructions on how to enforce the federal regulations. If parents refused to send their children to school the authorities could withhold annuities or rations or send them to jail. Some parents were uncomfortable having their children sent far away from home yet government educators had quotas to fill. Considerable pressure was exerted on Indian families to send their youngsters to boarding schools beginning when the child was six years old.

There have been several major legislative actions with regard to educating American Indians. The Snyder Act of 1921 authorized the federal government to provide special services to Indians. All American Indians were granted U.S. citizenship in 1924, regardless of whether they lived on tribally or privately owned land. However, in 1934, Congress passed the Indian Reorganization Act, which ceased allotments and re-institutionalized tribal governments. Under reorganization, it was possible to be a tribal citizen as well as a U.S. citizen. In addition, Congress passed the Johnson-O'Malley program in 1934, authorizing the federal government to contract with state and local governments to provide services to American Indians.

Coersive Assimilation

The Indian Reorganization Act of 1934 introduced the teaching of Indian history and culture in BIA schools, supplanting the Federal policy to acculturate and assimilate Indian people by eradicating their tribal cultures through a boarding school system. The Indian Self-Determination and Education Assistance Act of 1975 gave authority to federally recognized tribes to contract with the BIA for the operation of Bureau-funded schools and to determine education programs suitable for their children.

The Education Amendments Act of 1978 (and further technical amendments) provided funds directly to tribally operated schools, empowered Indian school boards, permitted local hiring of teachers and staff, and established a direct line of authority between the Education Director and the Assistant Secretary, Indian Affairs.

It wasn't until 1969, when the Special Subcommittee on Indian Education published Senate Report 91-501, commonly known as the Kennedy Report, that the federal government repented of its ugliness. Titled *Indian Education: A National Tragedy, A National Challenge*, it said: *"The dominant policy of the federal government toward the American Indian has been one of coercive assimilation"*, and the policy *"has had disastrous effects on the education of Indian children."*

The United States government publically admitted it made mistakes. While I was neither encouraged nor required to examine these kinds of bureaucratic and political details as a student teacher, the exposure was a revelation.

Navajo Nation History, A Brief Look

The Navajo Nation's recorded stories span a historical period from before the arrival of the Navajos in the Little Colorado River basin to the arrival of Euro-Americans, to the present. Appreciation for cultural heritage demands a look back beyond a generation or two. And let's be clear, a brief look at the history of the Navajo Nation won't explain the feeling of connectedness that emanates from being Navajo. It's complicated, ambiguous and difficult to describe. Being connected to one's culture involves pride, which results in skirmishes that are meant to protect and preserve one's freedom. Since Europeans landed on American soil, every Native American tribal community has experienced both big and small skirmishes, some of which turned into massacres, including the Navajo Nation.

Poet and philosopher George Santayana said, "Those who

cannot remember the past are condemned to repeat it." With that in mind, I'd like to add another tidbit—a brief summation of a dismal part Diné history commonly called The Long Walk.

The Long Walk

The Navajo had their first contact with Europeans in 1598. Spaniards had come north from Mexico bringing with them sheep and horses. The Spanish explorers tried to convert the Navajo people to their European customs and religion. According to author Raymond Friday Locke in *The Book of the Navajo*, "...they [the Navajo] were more interested in the Spaniard's sheep and horses." They resisted the Spanish, which according to historians such as Locke, allowed the United States government to capture and claim the southwest. This debt would not be formally repaid or even acknowledged.

When the Navajos tried to take advantage of the military slack caused by the outbreak of the Civil War, the U. S. government sent Colonel Kit Carson to settle the uprising. His mission was to gather the Navajo people and move them to Fort Sumner on the Bosque Redondo Reservation in New Mexico. When the Native Americans refused to move and hid in the Canyon de Chelly, he began a merciless genocidal campaign, destroying crops and livestock, burning villages and killing people. By destroying their food supplies, Carson eventually convinced the Navajos that going to the reservation was the only way to survive.

In 1864, Navajos, along with some other tribes, (eight to nine thousand people in all) began their move to Fort Sumner. According to David Roberts of the Smithsonian magazine, "Officials called it a reservation, but to the conquered and exiled Navajos it was a wretched prison camp." They were fed rations of rancid bacon and insect-infested flour, supplies that the U.S. Calvary troops were going to throw away.

The term The Long Walk refers to the 1864 deportation of the Native people, mostly Navajo, by the U.S. Government. Men, women and children were forced to walk at gunpoint to their "reservation" in Fort Sumner. The trip lasted for eighteen days. Finally, in 1868, the Diné were allowed to return to the Four Corners area, the land that they loved. They were coerced into signing a treaty in exchange for the land that would become the reservation they currently live on in the high desert of northwestern New Mexico.

Code Talkers

Conversely, Navajo history also teaches many noble heroic stories worthy of preservation. In the 1940's, for example, Navajo men bravely heeded the call of a nation—the same nation that nearly wiped out their ancestors and the memory of their culture completely. Twenty-nine young Marines of Navajo origin served as military "code talkers" in WWII.

Hollywood made a movie about it in 2002 called *Wind Talkers*. The film, directed by John Woo, was criticized for featuring the Navajo characters in supporting roles despite being the primary focus of the story. However, the film did manage to accurately depict events based on the genuine bravery of Navajo soldiers.

During the Second World War, the United States and its allies were struggling to find a code by which to communicate. The Japanese had been successfully cracking U.S. military code. A new secret language was needed. Since the Navajo language is one of the most difficult languages to master in the entire world, military officers decided to make use of this extremely complex language with no alphabet or symbols. To be able to speak Navajo, one must have extensive exposure and training.

Through the incredible linguistic skills attributed to the Navajo servicemen, the Allied forces were able to convey vital information to one another—information most leaders would say favorably altered the course of the war.

Traditional Navajo Worldview

In most cases, anthropocentric worldviews usually boast

a collection of stories that start with creation of the universe. A student of traditional Navajo culture might start with the Navajo creation story, which involves three underworlds where important events happened to shape the Fourth World where people now live. Suffice it to say, the mythical Navajo world is an orderly system of interrelated elements, hence the belief that everything is sacred and the steady development of seemingly innumerable taboos.

All of that to say, a community's view of the world and its origins often becomes the foundational element for their religious beliefs. Since religion is not just a set of beliefs but a way of life, Wil Yazzie had to make radical adjustments when he began to practice biblical Christianity.

Ceremonialism was the system Navajos created to cope with the dangers and uncertainties of their universe. As I witnessed, the majority of young Navajos believed sickness and misfortune were caused by supernatural agencies, the accepted cure for which was a prescribed ceremony. With the urbanization of more and more Native Americans, dependence upon ceremonies has perhaps waned since the 1950's and 60's when Wil was growing up. When Wil accepted Christ, he had to mentally and spiritually switch sides.

Traditional Navajo beliefs promote finding and preserving harmony with God's creation, which is a noble pursuit and should be maintained. However, when Wil examined the evidence, or the fruit of some of his other former beliefs, he concluded that much of the Navajo Nation's problems with suicide, alcoholism, drug abuse, incest, poverty, domestic violence and violence in general could be attributed to the acceptance of witchcraft among his people.

Cultural Empathy

Whether one studies Native Americans or Hoosiers from Indiana, homeless alcoholics, veterans, or celebrities, it becomes clear that each group retains a specific culture—and that culture defines them.

Having affection for one's culture is about feeling accepted. People want to belong to something, somewhere. If you take nothing else from this book, please remember that all of us want to belong to a compassionate group of some kind, whether it's a team, tribe, gang, or church. People need to be accepted, and it just so happens that the body of Christ is always looking for new members.

During the time I lived on the reservation, my capacity to empathize with a foreign, yet American, culture was an exotic blessing. Little did I realize that some thirty years later, my blessing would be greatly multiplied. Not only was I given the opportunity to retell the Yazzies' story, I was able to do so with a certain degree of familiarity. In the same way, Wil Yazzie could not have predicted that his extraordinarily brutal journey from addict to "fulfilled Navajo"—as he puts it—would be so remarkable that a former teacher turned writer from South Carolina would have no choice but to sit down and record it.

SHOCKING STATISTICS

Contrary to the notion that all Native Americans are alcoholics, or that they are just one drink away from becoming one, not all Native Americans have a drinking problem.

Exposing The Myth

Let's begin by dispelling the myth that Indians have a biological weakness for the effects of alcohol. Though some may disagree, according to Dr. Philip May, a professor of sociology and psychiatry and director of the Center for Alcoholism, Substance Abuse and Addiction at the University of New Mexico, "This myth has no basis in fact." Scientific studies had found Indians to metabolize alcohol at the same rate as non-Indians. However, it is no exaggeration to say that alcohol-related problems have and are continuing to undermine the cultural integrity of the Native American community.

> NOTE: The following information, though not intended to replace accepted research on the subject of alcohol and substance abuse on reservations, comes from the Robert Wood Johnson Foundation's Anthology: *To Improve Health and Health Care, Volume VI*, specifically "Combating Alcohol Abuse in Northwestern New Mexico: Gallup's *Fighting Back*

and Health Nations Programs" written by journalist turned politician Paul Brodeur.

Anheuser-Busch swag is everywhere on the reservation and elsewhere in Indian country. It's on everything from tee-shirts to reusable (but mostly disposable) party gear. Residents and visitors alike can't help but notice scores of delivery trucks covered front to back, side to side, with inviting realistic graphics of various thirst quenching products, the alcohol content ranging anywhere from 5% (Budweiser beer) to 40% (Bacardi Rum). Trash barrels filled to the brim with crumpled beer cans or broken brown-glass beer bottles, some pieces still held together by paper labels, is a common sight. Discarded cases strewn by the highway or piled up near cement picnic tables at a parking area are unmistakable evidence that fortunes have been made selling alcohol to Indians.

Profiteers

As reported by author Ian Frazier in his book *On The Rez*, John Jacob Astor, America's richest man in the early nineteenth century, amassed his original wealth from the furs-for-whiskey trading he did as the owner of the American Fur Company of New York City. Since then, and up until the present, beverage sales and distribution businesses have been notoriously successful when established near an Indian reservation in the southwest. As a result, the Navajo Nation has had it fair share of problems, but one key factor—other than easy access—has contributed to the abuse of alcohol on the reservation. Boredom, caused by a lack of employment and feelings of hopelessness, caused by an inferior educational system, has created a permanent underclass prone to abuse alcohol.

In the 1970's and 1980's, the rural northwestern corner of the state of New Mexico, namely San Juan and McKinley Counties and the town of Gallup in particular, had a frighteningly high rate of alcohol abuse. (This where Wil Yazzie spent much of his adulthood.) For years Gallup, New Mexico billed itself as the "Indian Capital of the World" because it served as the principal shopping center for thousands of Native Americans. Many individuals and families made it their regular routine to drive into the city on weekends from surrounding reservations.

But then something happened. When statistics revealed that alcohol abuse in Gallup had reached epidemic proportions, the city became infamously known as "Drunk Town, USA." By 1988, more than 34,000 people were being picked up each year for public intoxication and detained for up to twelve hours in the city's crammed and squalid drunk tank. (The drunk tank was conceived under a New Mexico protective custody program that started in 1973 after public drunkenness was decriminalized.) By comparison, just over 1,000 people were held in protective custody for drunkenness that same year in Albuquerque, 120 miles to the east, and Albuquerque had twenty times the population of Gallup.

Very few of those being picked up in Gallup were residents of the city. More than 90% of them were Native Americans, and they were mostly Navajos from the vast 25,000-square-mile Navajo Nation reservation. Detainees also included residents of the Zuni pueblo, the Acoma pueblo and the Laguna pueblo, all independent nations with sizeable Indian populations. Congress had repealed a federal law prohibiting the sale of liquor to Indians in 1953, but the Navajo, Zuni, Acoma and Laguna continued to ban liquor on their reservations.

As a result, Native Americans swarmed to Gallup to drink. During the next three decades, Gallup's economy was largely based not only on selling groceries, goods, and services to Native Americans but also on creating an environment that encouraged them to consume alcohol.

A Town Under the Influence

By 1987 sixty-one establishments in Gallup had been issued liquor licenses, which was more than five times the number allotted under a New Mexico law permitting only one license for every 2,000 inhabitants. Among them were twenty-five drive-up windows where one could buy liquor without leaving the car.

Wine fortified with brandy (to make it 19% alcohol) came into Gallup from California twice a month in tanker trucks, each carrying 5,500 gallons of the social lubricant. Many of the city's most prominent citizens owned bars, restaurants and liquor distribution outlets. These same individuals had also been elected to public office and appointed to various municipal and civic organizations. By 1987 the city of Gallup's liquor industry reported $142 million in sales—more taxable earnings than in the finance, insurance and real estate industries combined.

In addition to permitting easy access to liquor, Gallup had become a civic enabler for alcohol abusers in other ways. The city had twenty-one pawnshops (compared with 24 in all of Albuquerque), a blood plasma donation center, and two recycling centers, which gave problem drinkers a way to pick up quick and easy cash. Gallup also had three church-based soup kitchens and two free overnight shelters. Together with a revolving door protective custody program, which amounted to a free overnight stay in the Gallup jail, these facilities and programs offered little incentive for alcoholics to seek treatment for their disease.

The National Institute on Alcohol Abuse and Alcoholism (NIAAA) cited that as early as the mid-1970's, McKinley County was ranked as the worst of all counties in the United States for alcohol-related mortality. The mortality rate from cirrhosis was 2.3 times as high as the national average, the alcohol-induced mortality rate was 9.8 times as high, and the mortality rate from all alcohol-related causes was 3.7 times as high. For the three-year period, 1974 through 1976, the mortality rates of McKinley County residents for selected substance abuse-related causes were between 184 percent and 337 percent higher than those for New Mexico residents as a whole.

According to the NIAAA, McKinley County ranked first in the list of per capita deaths from chronic alcoholism, at nineteen times the nationwide rate. Alcohol-related homicides and suicides were three times the national rate. During the 1970's and 1980's, the county's drunken-driving death rate was seven times the U.S. rate. One out of every twenty licensed drivers in the county had received at least two drunken-driving citations since 1984. During the three-year period between 1986 and 1988, the county led the nation in motor vehicle deaths. Between 1983 and 1988, some 660 Navajos died on highways in northwestern New Mexico.

And yet statistics don't tell the whole story. Sometimes information has to become personal.

Navajo Nation Gets National Attention

After a three-month investigation, the *Albuquerque Tribune* published an article in May of 1988 wherein they stated Mother Teresa had added Gallup to her itinerary of "forsaken places." How can I add to that other than to say that after the officials of the Marin Institute for the Prevention of Alcohol and Other Drug Problems visited Gallup in 1989, they wrote:

> *In all our years of providing consultative and technical assistance to cities dealing with alcohol and drug-related problems, we have never encountered a situation as serious as that facing Gallup, the Native American reservations, and the surrounding region. We concur with the* Albuquerque Tribune's *assessment that Gallup is a 'town under the influence.'*

The magnitude of the problem had finally attracted regional and national media attention. Lengthy feature stories were produced by ABC's *20/20,* NBC's *Today Show,* and PBS's *On Assignment.* At the time, many citizens of Gallup responded with outrage, characterizing the accounts as unduly sensational and demanded that *Tribune* editors, reporters and photographers listen to their complaints. Two hundred of them attended a town hall meeting to vent their wrath. The mayor stood up and accused his citizens of being in denial, like many alcoholics, and challenged them to take action to improve the situation in Gallup instead of attacking those who had brought it to public attention.

Meanwhile, *Tribune* reporters interviewed every lawmaker heading to Santa Fe for the mid-January 1989 opening of the New

Mexico legislative session, asking what he or she thought the state could do to help Gallup resolve its alcohol crisis. The answers were discouraging, budgets were tight and the governor had just come out against raising taxes for any new programs or facilities.

The headline read, "No Hope Seen for Anti-Liquor Bills"—but that was just four days before a highway accident forever changed the attitude toward alcohol abuse in the lawmakers in Santa Fe, the residents of Gallup New Mexico and the awakening nation.

The Journey for Jovita

Late in the afternoon of January 14, a 32 year-old rodeo rider named Robert Christie, who had been drinking all day, left a Gallup bar with a bottle of vodka in his hand, climbed into his pickup truck, and headed south on a two-lane road toward the Zuni reservation. A short time later, he crashed head-on into a van carrying Kathleen Vega; her sister, Shirley Harry; her 12 year-old niece, Cheryl; and her infant daughter, Jovita. They were were on their way to a revival meeting.

Three-month-old Jovita was killed instantly, as were Shirley and Cheryl Harry. Christie, whose blood alcohol level turned out to be more than three times the legal limit, also died at the scene. Only Jovita's mother, Kathleen Vega, survived.

Outrage over the senselessness of the latest highway carnage spread through Gallup, McKinley County, and the Navajo and Zuni reservations. Starting on February 10, approximately 100 people started out on foot heading east on Interstate Highway 40, toward Albuquerque. Among them were Hispanics, Navajos, Zunis and other Native Americans, as well as many white residents of Gallup, including teachers, bankers and bureaucrats. Their numbers swelled along the way.

By the time the marchers reached Santa Fe, on February 20, their number had grown to more than 2,000. The mayor of Gallup reported it was the largest demonstration of its kind in New Mexico history. It caught the politicians by surprise. In a joint session of the House and Senate, Kathleen Vega spoke first then embraced Robert Christie's former wife, Marcie, who told the legislators that she had loved her husband but hated his disease. There wasn't a dry eye in the place.

New Mexico legislators then earmarked $300,000 to design a regional detoxification and rehabilitation clinic which would replace the Gallup's infamous drunk tank. They also enacted laws that prohibited open containers of alcoholic beverage in a motor vehicle, there would be no more drive-up windows for alcohol, and a 5% increase in the excise tax on liquor was passed.

Early in 1990, the Northwest New Mexico Council of Governments received an initial grant from the Robert Wood Johnson Foundation in the amount of $200,000 to develop a plan that would enable the three affected counties to participate in a program called Fighting Back: Community Initiatives to Reduce Demand for Illegal Drugs and Alcohol. As a result, citizens, health professionals, public officials and alcohol-reform activists were not only well-informed regarding the epidemic, but they were also able to tap into and create resources that dealt with underlying problems at all levels of the Native American community through education, treatment and prevention programs.

Some say the alcohol abuse situation in and around reservations has improved since the 1970's and 1980's. Others would disagree. There is still much work to be done.

Missionaries with a Message, Wil and Linda Yazzie

Wil and Linda work hard to combat substance abuse in the Four Corners Region. They understand that the underlying problems beneath addiction are often spiritual. They know from experience that when one has exhausted all other avenues for relief from addiction and the accompanying problems substance abuse creates, there's one resource that will be conspicuously omitted from government resources. Take God at His word, trust Him to heal the underlying causes of addiction, and like Wil, you will reap the rewards of being a child of God living for Christ.

DISCUSSION QUESTIONS

Chapter One CHILDHOOD INTERRUPTED

1.1. SAFE HAVEN Experts agree, children need to feel safe. What do you consider to be a safe haven? What makes it safe?

1.2. EXPECTATIONS What expectations do others have of you that make you uncomfortable or bring up feelings of resentment?

1. 3. NURTURE Who nurtures you? What are your gifts?

1.4. DIVORCE/POVERTY Has divorce or poverty affected your childhood? Has divorce or poverty affected someone you know?

Chapter Two GROWING UP NAVAJO

2.1. BAD PARENTS "Even bad parents are better than no parents." Do you agree or disagree with this statement? Explain.

2.2. CHANGE When a family experiences a major change, such as separation due to death, divorce or deployment, is there any way to prevent further harm?

2.3. BONDS What bonds are sacred to you?

Chapter Three OPEN DOORS OF ANOTHER KIND

3.1. ABUSE Whether the abuse is sexual, verbal or physical, children are deeply affected. What can a child do to cope?

3.2. TRUST What kind of incidents might cause you to have trust issues?

3.3. CRAVING What do you crave? What do you think triggers cravings?

3.4. BELIEFS What beliefs do you allow to control you?

3.5. ESCAPE What makes you want to escape?

3.6. NORMAL What is your definition of normal? What do you accept as normal that other people might not accept as normal?

3.7. VOWS What vows have you made and kept? What vows have you broken?

Chapter Four PLEASING THE ELDERS

4.1. MOTIVATION Actions are justified by motives. What action have you taken as the result of a specific motivation? Explain.

4.2. ADDICTIONS Often one addiction brings with it another. Addictions can start in childhood. If you had (or have) an addiction (not an obsession) that started in childhood, describe how it started. If you were able to overcome an addiction, explain how you were able to overcome your compulsion.

4.3. MIRACLES Have you experienced a miracle? Describe what happened and how it affected you.

4.4 PROMISES Has anyone ever made a promise to you and broken it? How did that affect your relationship?

4.5. PAIN Do you feel as though someone owes you and should pay for the pain they've caused you?

Chapter Five CAUGHT

5.1. ADDICTIVE BEHAVIOR How does a person act when they are feeding their addiction?

5.2. SELF IMAGE How you see yourself makes a difference. What do you do to boost your self-esteem?

5.3. FRIENDS Bad character corrupts good character. Do you agree with that statement? Explain.

5.4 GEOGRAPHY Do you think a change of geography (living arrangements) can help a person overcome challenges?

Chapter Six UNDER THE INFLUENCE

6.1. LONELINESS Do you find that you retreat into solitude on purpose? If so, does that good or bad? Describe how loneliness affects you.

6.2. SIN Do you believe sinful behaviors can control people like a master controls a slave?

6.3 CARING ADULTS Who are some of the most caring people you know? What have you noticed about them that indicates they are influencing people in positive ways?

6.4. ESCALATION Do you agree with the statement that addictive behaviors escalate? Explain.

6.5 TIRED OF IT What behaviors have you grow tired of, and what did you replace them with?

Chapter Seven CHILOCCO SCHOOL FOR INDIANS

7.1. FRUSTRATION When you get frustrated, do you behave badly? Have you tried to find ways of coping so you do not react poorly when things do not work out the way you had hoped?

7.2. SUCCESS Describe the first time you felt successful.

7.3. EMOTIONAL FUEL Make a list of your emotions, good and bad. Try to identify what is the driving force behind them.

7.4. "FRIENDS" Have you ever had friends use you to get what they want? Have you ever been that kind of a "friend?"

7.5. INDIANS On a scale of one to ten, how well informed are you when it comes to Native Americans? Use two scales, one for U.S. and Native American history and one for Native American customs.

Chapter Eight BREAKING RECORDS AND STUFF

8.1. MENTORS Have you had mentors in your life? If so, describe the relationship. If not, describe what you imagine a good mentor to be like.

8.2. GETTING CAUGHT Have you ever been caught doing the wrong thing? If so, how did you react? Did getting caught change you?

8.3. REJECTION Have you ever been rejected? If so, how did you handle it?

8.4. SHATTERED DREAMS Do you have dreams for your life? Have any of your dreams been destroyed? If so, did a person (or group of people) destroy them, or did a particular set of circumstances ruin your aspirations? Explain.

Chapter Nine CHRISTMAS IN OCTOBER

9.1. ILLNESS Have you ever experienced a life threatening illness or known someone who has? If you were diagnosed with a serious illness, how would you cope?

9.2. VISIONS Have you ever experienced a dream, or had a vision that affected you so deeply that it is still with you today? Have you, or would you share it with others?

9.3. PRAYER Do you know if anyone has ever prayed for you? If so, how did you find out? How do you feel about someone praying for you?

9.4. JESUS Who is Jesus to you?

9.5. FAVORITE THINGS Name ten of your favorites things. Have any of your favorite things carried over from your childhood?

Chapter Ten CONFINEMENT

10.1. HOME LIFE Would you say your home life was good? Describe your childhood using only three adjectives. Describe your present home life using only three adjectives.

10.2. BAD NEWS What do you do when you receive bad news?

10.3. BAD TEACHER Have you ever had a terrible teacher? If so, what made them a bad instructor?

10.4. FAITH As a child, did you have faith in God? If so, how strong was your faith? If not, do you wish that someone had provided religious instruction?

Chapter Eleven WHAT NOW

11.1. PEERS Do you influence your peers, or do your peers mostly influence you?

11.2. HABITS Do you have habits that you fall back into simply because they are comfortable? What are they? Are your habits mostly constructive or destructive?

11.3. PREMATURE DEATH Have you ever lost someone you cared about and realized his or her death was premature?

11.4. FIRST JOB Describe your first job. What did you learn from your first job?

11.5. DERELICTS What is your impression of derelicts—alcoholics, drug addicts, drug dealers, homeless people?

11.6. UNDER-AGED DRINKING What is your opinion about under-aged drinking? At what age do you feel people should be allowed to drink legally?

11.7. TOUGH TIMES How do you view tough times? Do you consider your challenges as opportunities to build character? Or do you self-medicate?

Chapter Twelve TRAPPED

12.1. PROTECTION Have you ever been protected? If so, what were you protected from, who protected you and how were you protected?

12.2. LIVING HELL Have you ever been trapped in what felt like a "living hell?" Did you have any way of escaping?

12.3. POINT OF NO RETURN Have you ever reached a "point of no return" and had to keep going? In other words, have you ever pursued something even when you knew the results weren't going to be good?

12.4. SCARED Have you ever been so scared that you were forced to make a significant change?

12.5. RIGHT AND WRONG In your life, has the line between right and wrong ever become fuzzy or hard to decipher? If so, can you describe the circumstances?

Chapter Thirteen FUGITIVE WANTED

13.1. CHAOS Have you ever had to deal with the chaos someone else created and left behind? Have you ever created chaos for someone else to deal with?

13.2. MERRY GO ROUND Have you ever been caught in a cycle, or felt trapped in circumstances that seemed impossible to overcome?

13.3. UNTHINKABLE Has anything unthinkable happened to you?

13.4. LESSONS NOT LEARNED Could you describe a lesson or two that you were taught but didn't learn? Exclude academic examples.

Chapter Fourteen ARRESTED AGAIN

14.1. GANGS Have you or a loved one ever been affected (or terrorized) by a gang or a gang member?

14.2. WON'T HAPPEN Have you ever thought "it won't happen to me."?

14.3. FIGHTING Have you ever been involved in a fight? What, if anything, is a good reason to physically attack someone?

14.4. ANGELS Have you ever had the impression that you've seen or had contact with an angel?

14.5. WRONGFULLY ACCUSED Have you or a loved one ever been wrongfully accused?

14.6. REPUTATION Do you have a reputation? What things have you done to create your reputation? Can you describe your reputation as others view it?

14.7. HARD HEART Would you say you are hard-hearted about some things? If so, what?

Chapter Fifteen SEEMED RIGHT AT THE TIME

15.1. SUPPORTERS Who are your supporters and how do they support you?

15.2. THRILLS What do you do for thrills?

15.3. CONSEQUENCES List five behaviors (actions) that have an immediate consequence. List five behaviors that have a definite consequence but are somewhat delayed. Can do you do things that have no consequence whatsoever?

15.4. GIVING UP Have you ever felt like giving up and known it was the right thing to do?

Chapter Sixteen COSTLY MISTAKES

16.1. LIFE WITH MEANING Can you describe a life with meaning?

16.2. HERITAGE Describe your heritage. How important is family to you?

16.3. SUPERNATURAL Has anything happened to you that you could label supernatural?

16.4. CLANS Who are your people? Do you respect your tribe?

16.5. BAD DECISIONS Out of all the bad decisions you've ever made, which one was the worst? Can you describe how it affected you? Did any of your bad decisions affect other people?

16.6. STRIPPED Have you ever been stripped of possessions, reputation, income, self-esteem?

Chapter Seventeen PEN PALS

17.1. NAIVE Have you ever been called naive? If so, would you agree with that assessment?

17.2. DATING What are your thoughts about dating?

17.3. SOUL MATES Do you believe in soul mates?

17.4. OBEY YOUR PARENTS Do you obey your parents? If not, why not? If so, are there exceptions when you would not abide by their decisions?

Chapter Eighteen NOTHING TO LOSE

18.1. DIVINE APPOINTMENTS Have you ever experienced coincidences and then thought they might have actually been divine appointments? Do you believe things happen for a reason?

18.2. BELIEVING IN YOURSELF Do you believe in yourself? If so, have you always had good self-esteem? If not, what would have to happen before you could believe in yourself?

18.3. DECEIVING YOURSELF Have you ever deceived yourself into believing something that was not true?

Chapter Nineteen DANGEROUS BUT SACRED GROUND

19.1. ROMANCE What is your definition of romance?

19.2. SCAMS Have you ever been a victim of (or been involved in) a scam?

19.3. JUDGE OF CHARACTER Are you a good or bad judge of character?

19.4. OPPOSITES ATTRACT Do you believe it's true that opposites attract? If so, is it a good thing?

19.5. INSPIRE OTHERS Have you ever inspired someone? Explain.

19.6. ATTRACTIVE What do you consider attractive?

Chapter Twenty MODEL PRISONER, BAD PAROLEE

20.1. FIRST IMPRESSIONS Do you make a good first impression? Do you think making a good first impression is important?

20.2. PLANNING FOR THE FUTURE Do you make plans for the future? If not, why not? If you think planning for the future is important, do you put your plans in writing, and if so, how far into the future do you plan—one year, five years, ten years? Have you ever thought about writing your obituary?

20.3. PLEASING OTHERS Do you live to please others, or yourself?

20.4. GOOD INTENTIONS Do you have good intentions but bad ideas?

20.5. EDUCATION Do you believe education makes a difference? Would you agree with the statement that inferior education is to blame for most of society's problems?

Chapter Twenty-One FAMILIAR SINS

21.1. TIMING IS EVERYTHING Would you agree with the statement that timing is everything?

21.2. BACKSLIDING When a person backslides and falls into sinful behavior, do you automatically condemn them, or do you try to help them? If you were an addict, how do you think you might react when and if someone tried to help you?

21.3. TEMPTATIONS What tempts you? How do you handle temptation? Do you think it is wise to be held accountable when you are struggling?

21.4. SPIRALING Have you ever spiraled out of control? If so, can you describe the circumstances?

21.5. BLINDERS Love covers a multitude of sins. Have you ever loved someone so much that you willingly put on blinders so the relationship could continue?

Chapter Twenty-Two CAN'T GIVE UP

22.1. CHOICES Have you ever had a hard time choosing between right and wrong?

22.2. LOVED ONES Have you ever disappointed a loved one?

22.3. UNSHAKABLE BELIEFS Do you hold any beliefs that you consider to be unshakable? If so, what are they? Why are they important to you?

22.4. FOUNDATIONS Do you have a strong foundation in life, one that is stable enough to build upon? If not, where are your weak links?

Chapter Twenty-Three REPEAT OFFENDER

23.1. INSTITUTIONALIZED Do you know what it means when someone says they feel institutionalized? Can you empathize or sympathize?

23.2. ACTIVIST Have you ever been an activist? If so, explain your motivation for doing so.

23.3. DOUBLE LIFE Have you ever felt as if you are leading a double life? Do you know anyone who leads a double life, and if so, do you think they are happy?

Chapter Twenty-Four WEAPON OF CHOICE

24.1. SHELTERED LIFE Do you know anyone who has led a sheltered life? If so, do you treat them with respect, or do you avoid them because they are different?

24.2. COMMUNICATE How do you prefer to communicate? If you were going to communicate something important, would do it verbally, or via a letter, text message or email?

24.3. FAVORITE BOOK Do you have a favorite book? If so, what is it? Explain how and why it affected you.

24.4. GET SAVED When a Christian uses the phrase "get saved," does it bother or offend you?

24.5. ADVERSITY Does adversity slow you down or paralyze you? Or does adversity bring out the best in you?

24.6. HUMILITY Are you a humble person? Do you consider people to be weak (or strong) when they show signs of humility?

24.7. FAITHFUL Have you ever been faithful (or unfaithful) to a cause, a person, or a calling?

Chapter Twenty-Five HOME SWEET HOME

25.1. RULER Are you the ruler of your own destiny? Do you let others rule over you? If so, in what ways do you let others control you?

25.2. DENIED Have you ever been denied something, such as a job, a promotion, a loan, etc? How do you react when you get the news that you've been denied?

25.3. MARRIAGE What are your views on marriage?

25.4. LYING Have you ever lied to get what you wanted or needed?

25.5. GOOD LIFE Describe your idea of "the good life."

25.6. EMOTIONAL ABUSE Have you ever been the recipient of emotional abuse? Have you ever been the abuser?

25.7. FAIRY TALE DREAMS Have you ever had dreams so big that they seemed unrealistic? Did you share them with other people? If so, what was their reaction?

25.8. BLAME Have you ever blamed others for things you know were your fault?

25.9. THINGS YOU CAN'T FORGET Make a list of the things that happened to you that you could never forget. Include the moments in your life that you will always remember.

25.10. SAVE A LIFE Have you ever saved someone's life?

Chapter Twenty-Six PRINCE NOT SO CHARMING

26.1. POWER OF LOVE Do you believe love changes people and/or circumstances?

26.2. SHAME Have you ever been shamed? If so, how did it affect you?

26.3. CONVICTIONS Do you have convictions that you hold dear to your heart? Is there anything you believe in so strongly that you would give up your life for it?

26.4. COMMON GROUND How important is it to you to have something in common with people? Make a list of your family members, friends and co-workers. Next to their name, write down things you have in common.

26.5. HIGH POWER Do you believe in a higher power? Explain.

26.6. SECRET DESIRES Do you have any secret desires?

26.7. MISTAKES Do you allow your mistakes to define you? When you fail, do you give up, or do you try again?

26.8. ENEMIES Do you have enemies? If someone hurts you, do you consider him or her an enemy? If so, explain.

Chapter Twenty-Seven WASTED YEARS

27.1. DESPAIR Have you ever been so desperate that you've done something regrettable?

27.2. CONSUMED Have you ever been consumed by something (or someone) wherein your life (or personality) became unbalanced?

27.3. ENABLERS Do you know any enablers? Have you enabled someone, making it possible for them to behave in an unhealthy fashion?

27.4. CRY FOR HELP Have you ever cried out for help? If so, did it work? Explain.

27.5. ENSLAVED Do you know what it feels like to be enslaved by an addiction? Do you believe addicts can recover?

Chapter Twenty-Eight WITHOUT WIL

28.1. CAREGIVERS Have you ever been a full or part-time caregiver? If so, was it a positive or negative experience?

28.2. ENCOURAGEMENT Do you mostly give or receive encouragement? Explain.

28.3. REBUILDING A LIFE Have you ever been in the position to rebuild your life? Have you ever helped someone rebuild his or her life?

Chapter Twenty-Nine GET RID OF HIM

29.1. UNWANTED Describe a time when you felt unwanted.

29.2. MENTALLY ILL Do you have any experience with people who are mentally ill? If so, can you describe how you handled (or viewed) their illness?

29.3. BULLIES Have you ever been bullied? Have you ever come to the realization that you were (or are) the bully?

29.4. CHEATING DEATH Have you ever been on the brink of death? If so, did it change you? Explain.

Chapter Thirty TRANSITIONS

30.1. DEATH OF A LOVED ONE Have you lost a loved one? How did you cope?

30.2. ISOLATED Have you ever felt isolated? Was your isolation physical, emotional or spiritual?

30.3. WORLDVIEW What is your worldview? In other words, do you have a certain philosophy of life that influences everything you do?

30.4. PRETEND Have you ever discovered that you pretend to be someone other than yourself? In other words, do people know the real you?

30.5. LEADERSHIP Have you ever started a program, or opened a business, or taken a leadership position of any kind?

30.6. ADVICE What is the best (worst) advice you've been given? What is the best (worst) advice you've given to someone?

Chapter Thirty-One ACTING IS AN ART

31.1. ADMIRE What and whom do you admire? Explain.

31.2. NEW DIRECTIONS Has your life ever taken a completely new direction? Describe how it came about.

31.3. SPOTLIGHT Are you comfortable in the spotlight? If so, under what circumstances?

31.4. ADVOCATE Are you an advocate of something or someone? Explain.

31.5. TRIGGERS If you are (or have been) addicted to something, do you know what your triggers are? What (sounds, sights, smells, situations, emotions) will activate your addiction? For example, is it hunger, anger, loneliness, fatigue, or is it a person, place, or thing?

Chapter Thirty-Two LAST CHANCE

32.1. BAND AIDS When a situation becomes challenging, do you tend to find a temporary, short-term solution (a band aid), or do you try to find a long-term, permanent solution?

32.2. ROCK BOTTOM Have you ever hit rock bottom? Have you ever felt hopeless? Explain.

32.3. PLAYING GAMES Could you admit to yourself and others that you've been played games instead of being a genuine person? Have you ever played games with God?

32.4. BIBLE STORIES Do you read the Bible, and if so, do certain Bible stories impress you? Which Bible stories have helped to shape you or have caused you to consider things from a different perspective?

Chapter Thirty-Three ALL THESE THINGS

33.1. APOLOGIES Do you know the difference between an artificial apology and a sincere apology? Using a familiar situation, can you give an example of both types of apologies? Have you ever offered a sincere apology and it was not accepted? Have you ever offered an artificial apology?

33.2. FORGIVENESS Are you able to extend and receive forgiveness? If not, why not?

33.3. REMARRIAGE What is your opinion on multiple marriages? What do you think about people who remarry each other?

33.4. COMMITMENT What kinds of commitment do you make on a regular basis? Have you ever been asked to make a commitment and refused? Have you ever made a commitment and let someone down? Explain.

33.5. CALLING Do youi know what it means to be called of God? Do you feel that you have a calling from God? If so, do you share it with others, or do you keep it to yourself?

33.6. STEPPING OUT ON FAITH Have you ever done something that requires a great deal of faith? If so, how did you come to have such faith? Explain.

Chapter Thirty-Four TOTAL FORGIVENESS

34.1. MEMORIES How do you deal with unpleasant memories?

34.2. PURPOSE Do you lead a purpose-driven life? If not, why not?

34.3. HEARING GOD Rather than an audible voice, most people are comfortable acknowledging that God speaks to them by making a distinct impression in their hearts and minds, which they then verbalize. Has God every spoken to you?

34.4. WITCHCRAFT Have you ever been exposed to witchcraft? If so, explain the situation and your response.

34.5. TABOOS Do you subscribe to any taboos or spupertitions (flawed thinking)? In other words, have you ever told yoursel the following: *If ___ happens, then ___ will happen as a result?*

34.6. SPIRITUAL WARFARE Christians believe God is good and his enemy, Satan, is evil. As a result, there is a constant battle for our eternal souls. Do you agree or disagree with this statement?

Chapter Thirty-Five RECOVERY

35.1. LOVE "We are shaped and fashioned by what we love." Do you agree or disagree with this statement? Explain.

35.2. STAMINA What kind of staying power do you have with regard to your physical life? What kind of stamina do you have with regard to your spiritual life?

35.3. COMPASSION Do you think people make improvements when they are shown compassion? Is it more likely someone will become a bad citizen if they have not experienced compassion?

35.4. PROMPTED Have you ever had an overwhelming feeling that came upon you that caused you to do something or say something out of the ordinary?

35.5. CULTURE How important is it for you to retain your culture? Explain.

35.6. RESTORATION Do you believe God is involved when someone's reputation, damaged relationship, or fortune is restored? Or do you believe people are solely responsible for everything that happens, good and bad?

35.7. RECOVERY PROGRAMS Do recovery programs work? Why, or why not?

35.8. DAILY HABITS Do you do anything on a daily basis that you consider to be a healthy (unhealthy) habit?

If you would like to know more about how you can be set free from addiction, or would like to contact Wil and Linda, you can email them at

wilandlinda@totalpardon.com.

Both Wil and Linda are available for speaking engagements. For updates on their ministry and other related news, please visit

www.totalpardon.com.

If you would like to contact Jodie Randisi, you can email her at

jodie@totalpardon.com.

Jodie is available for speaking engagements. If you have an amazing true story, you may contact **jodie@do-the-write-thing.com**

COWCATCHER

p u b l i c a t i o n s

Made in the USA
San Bernardino, CA
10 June 2015